How to
BUY
BUS

How to BUY A BUSINESS

The Daily Telegraph Guide

Peter Farrell

Kogan Page

Copyright © Peter Farrell 1983
All rights reserved

First published in Great Britain in 1983
by Kogan Page Ltd
120 Pentonville Road
London N1 9JN
Reprinted with revisions 1985, 1986, 1987

British Library Cataloguing in Publication Data
Farrell, Peter
   How to Buy a Business
   1. Entrepreneur — Small Business
   I. Title
   338.0'42   HB615

   ISBN 0-85038-634-9 Hb
   ISBN 0-85038-635-7 Pb

Printed and bound in Great Britain by
Billings & Sons Limited, Worcester

Contents

National Westminster knows a lot about small businesses

We can help you if you wish to expand your business

Our venture capital scheme for small businesses — the Capital Loan Scheme — is unique.

We are participating jointly with the Department of Industry in the Government Loan Guarantee Scheme.

We can help you if you are setting up in business

Our Business Development Loans are specially tailored for the growing small business and are appropriate for both working capital needs and for investment in new fixed assets.

We can provide a whole range of other services...

including unrivalled advice and information.

Do you receive free our Small Business Digest?

All you have to do is to contact your local NatWest Manager. He's there to help you.

NatWest Services for Small Businesses

Introduction

This is a book for the small businessman. City whizz-kids and captains of industry will find little here to interest them. That is not to say that the small business operates under different rules or lives in a different world from the large business; on the contrary, it can learn a lot from the way that big business thinks and works — a successful small business will, after all, become a larger business.

But the person buying a business for the first time, or even the established small firm expanding by acquiring another undertaking, has neither the experience, nor the access to expensive advice, which is available to more substantial businesses. The fact that, in such cases, the purchase of a business is likely to be a critical step, perhaps involving the staking of a whole career or a lifetime's savings, makes it all the more important that there should be some guidelines within which to take decisions. This book sets out to provide them.

The assumption throughout the book is that the reader is considering buying a business which he or she intends to run personally and, at the lower end of the scale at least, that factors other than strictly commercial criteria may be important. In other words, the book is based on the premise that the reader wants to own a business because he wants not just the financial rewards but also the satisfaction, excitement and fun of managing it.

Though it is assumed that the reader knows something about the line of business in which he is interested — it would take a very large book to cover all the skills that might be needed to run a butchery business, say, or a small engineering factory — it is not taken for granted that he is familiar with accountancy terms or even quite basic financial management. Experience suggests that a poll of even fairly substantial and successful small businessmen would reveal a surprising number who would be hard pressed to interpret another business's accounts correctly.

Finally, it is not suggested that this book is a substitute for proper professional advice: quite the contrary. A shrewd accountant, an efficient solicitor, even a sympathetic bank manager, are indispensable sources of help, information and expertise and it would be foolhardy to take a major step like buying a business without involving them at every stage. But the value of professional advice not only depends upon the quality of those who give it, it also hinges upon the ability of those who receive it to understand and interpret it. Rather than helping or encouraging readers to dispense with advice, therefore, the book is intended to enable them to make the best use of it.

Although every effort has been made to ensure that the text of this revised reprint was correct at the time of going to press, it may be that subsequent budget changes will affect some of the figures quoted and the reader should, if in any doubt, check to make sure that he has taken account of these.

Chapter 1

Why Buy?

There are, it is said, three ways of acquiring a fortune: inheriting it, marrying it or making it. All three methods can be used just as well to come by a business but, unlike fortunes, businesses can also be bought. It is probably a bit late to do anything about inheritance, and this book has no hints to offer on the wooing of heiresses, so if you want your own business we will assume that you have a choice between creating it from scratch or buying it — more or less — ready made.

In some cases, of course, the choice makes itself. If you have a completely new product to make or sell, then you will not, by definition, be able to buy a business that is already active in your line; conversely, if you have set your heart on running a shop in the local High Street, then you will probably have to buy or rent an existing store. But, assuming that your ambition is to have, say, a builder's business, an estate agency or a furniture factory, what are the pros and cons of buying a going concern as opposed to building a business from the ground up?

For many people who hope to go into business on their own, the advantages of buying seem overwhelming — and they may well be so. But this first chapter is by way of being a cautionary word to the impatient, for one ancient rule should constantly be borne in mind by anyone contemplating purchasing a business, *caveat emptor*: let the buyer beware.

Hasten slowly

The first apparent advantage of buying is speed. You are in business from the word go, with premises, equipment, labour, suppliers and customers. The cash is flowing in and out of your bank account and you can get on with the job of running the business to the best advantage. You don't have to waste time looking for suitable sites, choosing equipment, recruiting staff, negotiating with suppliers or creating a clientele. The attraction seems obvious: why waste time painstakingly digging the foundations and laying the bricks when there is a brand new house round the corner ready to move into?

The problem is that buying a business is not like buying a new house, a new car or a stereo. Any business you buy is, by its very nature, second-hand. It will have been built up, or at the least substantially modified, by its previous owner to suit his tastes, interests and prejudices, which may not be the same as yours. If it doesn't work the way you expected, or has unforeseen flaws, you cannot call in the builder to remedy them, or take it back to the shop and ask for a new one. You are going to have to make the best of it.

If the premises turn out to be in the wrong place, or hideously inconvenient for your purpose, you will have to live with them. Even if you got the machinery or the fittings at a knock-down price, they may turn out to be a liability rather than an asset; it may be more costly to take them out and replace them than it would have been to buy new ones at the outset. Moreover, as we shall see in a moment, you cannot necessarily assume that the customers will stay with you.

The track record

The second advantage of buying an existing business is that you have a track record to go on. You can look at past sales figures and accounts and see what turnover the business has had and how much profit it has generated. This may be a source of reassurance to your bank manager and your accountant as well as a comfort to yourself.

But the problem with records is that, while they tell you what has happened in the past when the business belonged to someone else, they do not tell you what is going to happen in the future when it belongs to you. Moreover, business records can conceal as much as they reveal, and it may take a very skilled eye indeed to discern the rickety structure behind the impressive facade. This applies particularly, as we shall see in Chapter 4, in the case of small businesses, where the results that go into the records may depend a great deal on the whims, the needs and the life-style of the owner. What you read may be perfectly accurate as far as it goes, but it may be very far from the whole story.

The owner

What applies to the hard, ascertainable facts applies even more

THINKING OF AUTOMATING YOUR OFFICE?

Then you may wish to receive **Mind Your Own Business** *free* each month and learn about micro computers, word processors, speech and data communications and all the products and services that go together in todays efficient office.

Complete and return the coupon and we will send you a sample copy of the magazine and if it proves as useful to you as it does to our existing 50,000 readers then we will invite you to register with us to receive copies each month at *no charge*.

Please send me a free sample copy of Mind Your Own Business

Name _____ Position _____

Company_____

Address_____

_____

Tel. No. _____ Date _____

Mind Your Own Business 106 Church Road London SE19 2UB

forcefully to the imponderables. Most small businesses, and many large ones, are very much a matter of personality — the personality of the owner above all. A shop may flourish because the shopkeeper builds up a clientele who buy there out of personal friendship and loyalty as much as from need or convenience; a local builder may flourish because of personal contacts, knowledge of the district and his membership of the Rotary Club rather than because of the quality of his work or the competitiveness of his prices. You, a stranger to the area, cannot assume that the existing customers or contacts will like you or you them. It may take time for you to find your way around the neighbourhood, socially and geographically, and you may heartily dislike the Rotary Club. The track record that looked so steady and predictable on paper may turn out to have been an ephemeral creation of one man's character rather than a guarantee of future success. Of course, you can build up your own contacts, find new customers, set a different, perhaps better, style. But in that case, you are in essence building up a new business, and the fact that you are, perforce, building it on the foundations of an old one may turn out to be a drawback rather than an advantage.

Making changes

The fact is that any business which has been going some time will have become set in its ways, and altering them can be hard, time-consuming and frustrating work. The previous owner may have got good service from a supplier because he spent a lot of time in the pub with his rep — not much help if you find the pub and the rep tedious; it may involve a good deal of agony to persuade the foreman in your newly acquired factory, or the assistant in your shop that, just because old Mr So-and-so always did something this way, it need not be the best way to do it.

In other words, you will almost certainly find a good many things in your new business which you do not agree with or approve of, and changing them may involve a good deal more patience and compromise than you have reckoned on. Unless you are buying a very big business indeed, sitting at your desk and writing a peremptory memo won't solve the problem. However much you may know about your trade in theory, *you* are going to be the new boy in this business, even if you are the boss; and human nature being what it is, your staff, your customers and your suppliers are likely to see every innovation and improvement you want to make as a turn for the worse. It is up to you to cajole, persuade and demonstrate that your way may indeed be better, easier, more efficient or more profitable.

Advantages of buying

Having established that buying a business — any business — is a project to be approached with caution and scepticism, let us now turn to some of the factors that can make it a prudent and profitable step. The first thing to look out for in any purchase may be the unexpected snags; the second is certainly the opportunities it presents.

Changing direction

Unlike a business which you have built up (which we will assume would be run at the peak of efficiency), a business which you are thinking of buying may well be free-wheeling along with a good deal of scope for improvement. That cash flow which is one of its immediate advantages might, with energetic management, be made to flow a good deal faster; the premises and the equipment may be inefficiently used or badly laid out, a possibility which you, the outsider, are ideally placed to spot. The present owner may be stuck, from force of habit or loyalty, with expensive or old-fashioned suppliers; he may be wedded to a shrinking sector of the market or an ageing clientele, matters which you, as a new broom, will be able to sweep clean.

The trick will be to capitalise on the sound aspects of the business — a skilled staff, say, an established name or a good location — while at the same time introducing new ideas or developing in a new direction. This is very often the case when a business is up for sale because the owner has reached retirement age; he may have a shop on a good site which is under-exploited because he has not perceived how the neighbourhood has changed and has not kept pace with its needs and tastes. Or it may be a factory with a good site and a skilled work force which has become run down and its equipment outdated because the owner, consciously or unconsciously, refused to keep up with changing methods, markets or technology. Providing you do not pay over the odds for the outdated shopfittings or the machines that are fit only for the scrap-heap, you may well be able to turn a static or declining business into a go-ahead expanding one much more quickly than you would be able to start a new undertaking from scratch.

Scrutinising the finances
The accounts, too, may conceal opportunities just as easily as they hide profits. Most notoriously, since the asset stripping era of the late sixties, property may be undervalued; even if you do not want to buy simply in order to sell again at a profit, it may provide just the security you need in order to borrow for expansion, or it may be that redevelopment or restoration would dramatically improve its worth. But it is not only the property values you should look out for. It may be that the over-large sums owed by debtors could be collected more rapidly with aggressive credit control and dramatically improve the liquidity; or that gross profit could leap with modern equipment and less labour, or the net profit improve with more up-to-date office equipment or better control of overheads.

Owner's personality
Just as the personality of the owner may have been an asset which you cannot replace, it may equally have been a handicap which, once removed, will enable the business to advance by leaps and bounds. A surly or unwelcoming shopkeeper may have kept people out of the premises; a hidebound or over-cautious manager may have held back a manufacturing business; a greedy or uninterested owner may have simply starved an enterprise of funds or energy. If you have the right personality, the business talent and the will to win, you may be able to do a very great deal better than your predecessor.

Your own personality is a factor you must consider if you are weighing up the pros and cons of buying a business. There are people with traits — an obsession with detail, an unwillingness to compromise, a wish to have things exactly their way — which are a big handicap when it comes to taking over a going concern, where the important thing may be to get the broad approach right before worrying about trivia, where compromise may be vital in the short term at least, and where the incoming owner is going to have to settle for adapting and reshaping someone else's creation rather than tearing it down and rebuilding it.

There are also many people with exactly those talents which are required to leap into the driving seat of a business while it is on the move and get the very best out of it. They have a

kind of sixth sense, or perhaps just a very clear mind, which enables them to see where the bottlenecks in the enterprise are occurring, and the persuasive skills to make other people see things their way without offending them. Their skill is more akin to that of a deft mechanic, who repairs and tunes the machine to perfect running order rather than of the creator who designs and builds it.

Recognising the problems
Even when there is patently something very wrong with a business, there may be a certain advantage in buying it — at the right price, naturally — rather than trying to start up a similar one. It may be that the problem is one that you can spot and feel confident you can remedy, in which case the business, once you own it, will have the advantage of a costly lesson learnt at someone else's expense. The problem you can identify so clearly when it is set out in black and white in the previous owner's accounts might not have been nearly so obvious to you if it grew up insidiously right under your nose, and drastic surgery on someone else's creation may be a lot less painful and traumatic than taking the knife to your own. Cutting losses is never pleasant, but it is a lot easier if they are someone else's.

Buying any business is inevitably a matter of buying a pig in a poke: the pig may lie down and die tomorrow, or it may grow up into a champion, but at least there is a pig there and you can see bits and pieces of it through the bars; for many people, buying it will be preferable to trying to breed their own pig. This book is intended for those who have decided in principle to take the plunge and buy a business. It sets out to help you spot the snags as well as to see the possibilities; to provide a key to interpreting the business's past record; to clarify what you are buying and what you can and can't do with it; and last, but not least, show where to raise the money to pay for it.

Chapter 2

Why is it for Sale?

When you find a business up for sale which looks like a real possibility, the first thing to ask yourself is, 'Why is it on the market?' If it is really as solid, profitable and full of potential as the vendor claims, surely he would be a fool to let it go at any price. The vendor has no obligation to provide the real, or indeed any, reason for selling the business and, unless the explanation is one which is patently accurate, such as ill-health or old age, you should certainly not take it at face value.

The vendor's real motive for selling can be a factor, not only in calculating the real value of the business, but also in determining what sort of deal may hold most appeal for him. For example, a proprietor whose creditors are beating on the door will obviously settle only for as much cash on the nail as he can get. On the other hand, someone selling a business and going into retirement may well (as we shall see later in this chapter) consider, even prefer, a series of payments spread over a period of years.

The owner who is selling because he has to is naturally in a weak position which you, as a potential purchaser, can take advantage of. But before you rush in for the kill you must assure yourself that you are not going to follow in his footsteps; in particular be wary of businesses which have changed hands frequently. In the case of a shop this may mean that the site is just wrong; even if a business is basically sound, one consequence of a series of changes of ownership may be that the stuffing has simply been knocked out of it by repeated switches of policy or management. Beware of such lame ducks; it may be that you, unlike the earlier owners, can get it right — but it may also be that the problems are fundamental or the damage irreversible.

Even in the case of an apparently booming business, it is a rash buyer who assumes that the present owner is telling the whole truth when he says that, having made his pile, he is retiring to a life of luxury and ease. That may be so; it may also be the case that the astuteness which made the pile has also suggested the right moment to get out, before the bubble bursts. It is vital to remember that the person selling the business inevitably knows a good deal more about it than the person buying it.

Owner's retirement

The commonest reason of all for small businesses coming on to the market is probably the wish of the owners to retire because of old age or ill-health. This is, happily, the circumstance in which it is easiest for the prospective purchaser to accept the explanation at face value. It is also, however, the case that businesses whose owners are about to retire should be looked at with particular circumspection. There is no doubt that, especially in the case of very small businesses where the management may effectively consist of the owner alone, there will have been a temptation to let the business run down as the prospect of retirement loomed larger. Indeed, the date of retirement may have been determined by business circumstances — the expiration of a lease, for example — which the outgoing owner did not face up to on the grounds that present arrangements would at least 'see him out'.

A business which has been built up by one owner over a long period, and which has become set in its ways, is particularly prone to have grown old along with its proprietor. He may have stuck to old-fashioned methods, old-established customers, an ageing labour force, without having any incentive to think very far into the future. Even in a larger business, such as a medium-sized private company which has been built up by its founder, there may have been an unexpressed desire to see the company die with its founder's departure — thus proving his indispensability. Such a feeling probably will not have been expressed in an overt attempt to actually sabotage a future owner's chances, but it may well have caused the outgoing owner to ignore potential problems or postpone important decisions on the grounds that the repercussions would not be felt in his time.

Clearly, a prospective purchaser will look at such moribund businesses with a particularly sceptical eye. If the fundamentals of the business are right — a good site for a shop, say, or a firm hold on a particular specialised market — then new management may be able to revitalise the business rapidly and achieve dramatically improved results. But if the basics are wrong — the business is involved in a declining trade, for example, or is equipped with out-of-date machinery — or if the slide has simply gone too far, then there may be little that a new broom can do except sweep up the debris. The points to watch out for in a business like this are relatively easy to spot.

Is the line of business sound?

It is perfectly possible that Town Centre Typewriters has provided its owner with a comfortable income for the past 40 years, but if, around the end of the sixties, he failed to come to terms with the transistor and simply carried on selling and servicing the adding machines and manual typewriters he knew and understood, then the prospects for the business may now look distinctly gloomy. Whether it has a future or not largely depends upon whether the gaping hole in the local market has already been filled by an existing shop or a newcomer. If Hi-Street Hi-Fi has spotted the opening and cornered the market for calculators and electric typewriters, and hired staff to service them, then Town Centre Typewriters will die with its owner's retirement unless you have been foolish enough to take over from him.

Is the business a sound proposition?

If the market is there for the product concerned, it doesn't follow that the business itself is a sound proposition. Suppose that you have been offered a chance to buy Parfit Printing Ltd from old Mr Parfit who has served the jobbing printing needs of a medium-sized town for the past 50 years. There is no doubt that the demand for wedding invitations, headed stationery, advertising leaflets etc is greater than ever. But look at Mr Parfit's business a little more carefully. His equipment consists of a couple of linotype machines circa 1930 and a flat bed press of about the same vintage ('They don't make them like that any more,' Mr Parfit will assure you, patting the lovingly tended machines) and these are operated and maintained by Fred Fount and Sid Serif who have been working for Mr Parfit since the war ('You can't find craftsmen like Fred and Sid any more,' Mr Parfit laments, 'Young people these days don't have the patience.'). In fact, Fred, Sid and their machines are relics of a bygone age and the first youngster out of technical college who sets up with a modern photosetting machine and a small litho printing press will price them out of the market in a few months. If you are intent on getting into the local printing business you will find that youngster and install him and his equipment in new premises rather than facing the problem of dismantling Mr Parfit's antiques and persuading Fred and Sid that the time has come for them to retire.

In short, you must reassure yourself that the business you are interested in has been run with an eye to the future rather than the past and that the owner has not allowed it to lose its impetus and edge.

How will the business be sold?

Assuming that none of these snags exists, you can pass on from the question of why the owner wants to sell his business to how — if the motive is impending retirement — he wants to sell it. Like anyone else, he doubtless wants to get the best price he possibly can; in Chapter 6 we shall be looking at how to assess what you, as a purchaser, should pay. The fact that he is about to become an old age pensioner certainly should not influence what you pay, but it may affect how and when you pay it.

Anyone selling a business, or a substantial part of one, is likely to be affected by *capital gains tax*. Leaving aside the case of a limited company for the moment, and restricting ourselves to sole traders and partnerships, the fixed assets of the business — which are all that is being sold (see Chapter 3) — have a book value which represents their original cost less (in the case of equipment or stocks) any amounts that have been written off as depreciation. When the owner of those assets sells them, he is liable to pay capital gains tax on the difference between the book value and the price he receives. In the case of even a modest business which has been going for some time such gains can be very substantial. This is especially so in the case of land or property; though this is not written down or depreciated in value but carried forward in the accounts at cost, its value will almost certainly have vastly increased over the years.

The point about capital gains tax for our present purpose is that there are special concessions designed to help those who have built up a business over the years and wish to realise their assets when they retire. Rates and thresholds vary from budget to budget, but currently (1985) no one has to pay CGT provided they keep their capital gains below £5600 a year (this is, by the way, a net figure and thus a capital gain of £7600 would still escape the taxman's net if it was offset by a capital loss of £2000 in the same year). But in the case of someone who has reached the age of 60, when the gain is the result of selling assets of a business which he has owned for at least ten years, the threshold is raised to £20,000 in any one year and to a cumulative total of £100,000. This provision obviously makes it advantageous for a vendor who has reached the age of 60 and whose business assets are likely to realise a capital gain of more than £20,000 to spread the sale of them over two or more years, and thus avoid paying CGT.

Here is a rare instance where the interests of both vendor and purchaser coincide. The purchaser, naturally, would like to pay for his purchase as slowly as possible, and it is in the vendor's interests to receive payment in annual instalments as well. The danger is that such an arrangement may encourage both parties to succumb to a temptation that is often damaging, to have some kind of 'handing over' or familiarisation period during which control of the business is shared. Given that the retiring owner is almost bound to see himself as the experienced, mature manager who could still teach the youngsters a thing or two, and that the incoming owner is equally likely to see himself as a modern, energetic whizz-kid, itching to straighten out the archaic follies of an old fogy, it is not surprising that such arrangements usually result in hard feelings all round and are damaging to the business itself. This is a circumstance in which accountants and lawyers can justify their fees by devising a scheme which permits a clean transfer of control while safeguarding the interests of the outgoing owner and making sure that both sides get a fair share of the advantage which the tax concession offers.

Where a limited company is concerned, things are not so simple. As explained in Chapter 3, the purchaser is buying either the assets of the company (when the company rather than its owners incurs the liability for CGT) or the company itself (in which case the shareholders' capital gain is the difference between the price they paid for the shares and the price they sell them for); more complicated rules apply when shares in a company acquired before 1964 are involved.

Although impending retirement is certainly one of the most common reasons for selling a small business, there are a few cases here and there of owners who — very wisely — face up to the fact that they are temperamentally unsuited to be running a business of their own. Through hard work and a dogged sense of duty they have managed to keep their businesses in the black, but they have come to the conclusion that the personal price they are paying is just too high. Perhaps they have realised that they lack the kind of energy and commitment which is so vital to the success of a small business, or maybe they feel their nerves are not up to coping with the many strains and responsibilities inherent in owning, say, an upholstery shop. They may, in fact, want to quit the rat race altogether and opt for premature retirement in the South Pacific.

If you are confronted with the opportunity of buying from such vendors, peruse their past years' accounts very carefully indeed to ensure that their emotional ambivalence has not led the business into financial instability. On the other hand, their eagerness to sell and rid themselves of what they consider an awkward burden can often work to your advantage, especially if their dislike of the business has not outweighed the demands of conscientious management.

Small business, large owner

At the other end of the spectrum from the small man retiring after a lifetime's work building up a business is the large corporation seeking to dispose of a small subsidiary. Large companies frequently have such unwanted foundlings in their care for a variety of reasons: they may have belonged to some larger business which was taken over; they may be the result of some past enthusiasm for diversification which has now evaporated; or the parent may simply want to raise cash by selling off an undertaking that is, from their point of view, peripheral. Whatever the reason given, prospective purchasers should look on large companies offering bargains with the same scepticism as the ancient world looked upon Greeks bearing gifts.

Almost by definition, such a business is for sale because the parent company has been unable to make it yield a sufficient profit, or, even worse, it has been milked so dry of any profit that might be obtained that there is nothing left. If you are offered an opportunity to buy, say, this splendid little engineering business which, says the vendor, eyes brimful of crocodile tears, no longer 'fits in with the group's long-term corporate strategy' but is an ideal opportunity because 'Small men like you can teach us big boys a lot about running this kind of business', grit your teeth and look the gift horse firmly in the mouth; the point of the metaphor, you will recollect, is that you can tell a horse's age by inspecting its teeth.

What happened to a subsidiary in the care of a larger parent is every bit as relevant to a would-be buyer as the age of a horse. All too often the small subsidiary will have been run, not in its own interests but in those of its owners. You should discover as much as possible about two areas: how the parent has treated its dependant's business and its assets, and how it has manipulated the accounts.

The most straightforward instance is the company whose assets have been blatantly 'stripped'. Take the hypothetical case of Mizzen & Boom, the old family firm of yacht builders (est 1910). Five years ago, when the last Mr Mizzen battened down his hatches for retirement (the original Mr Boom died childless so the business had become the sole property of the Mizzen family) this was exactly the kind of medium-sized, efficient and go-ahead business you are looking for now. But at the time you were not around and Mizzen & Boom was sold to Universal Leisure Ltd, the sporting goods conglomerate which made a number of portentous and totally insincere statements about the 'tremendous opportunities which exist for a business like this within the framework of our diversified enterprise'. What Universal Leisure then did was to sell Mizzen & Boom's boatyard — which was ideally situated near the centre of a fashionable yachting resort — to their own holiday camp subsidiary at a knock-down price, and transferred the yacht building work to a polluted and malodorous creek ten miles away. They sold the patent rights in a new dinghy on which the business had been working for ten years to their arch rivals, Tiller & Jib, for cash, most of which went to Universal Leisure by way of 'finders' fees', commission and management and accountancy charges; moreover, they refused to invest in new equipment or to continue Mizzen & Boom's apprenticeship scheme. Universal Leisure have now put the business on the market again, explaining that their new policy is to concentrate resources on developing holiday resorts in Belize. There is, of course, virtually nothing left of Mizzen & Boom except the name, the labour force is demoralised and troublesome, the skilled managers and designers left long ago having seen the way the wind was blowing, its product range is out of date and its customers have deserted. In short, every one of Mizzen & Boom's assets which could be converted into cash has been converted, the money has found its way to the coffers of

Universal Leisure, and all that is left is a husk which has been sucked dry.

The destruction of a small business by a giant owner does not have to take the form of outright looting of this kind; much more insidious and harder to detect, though almost as damaging, is the process of chopping and changing to which many subsidiaries are subjected. Probably the central management of the group only recollects that it is actually responsible for the business once or twice a year, and if there are problems its reaction is to treat the symptoms by swift, dramatic surgery without any attempt to make a full diagnosis. The treatment often takes the form of despatching a new managing director to sort things out — the chances are that the new man is a whizz-kid intent on carving a way up the corporate hierarchy who sees the appointment as a stepping stone to a better job at head office or, equally disastrous, an executive who has failed to make the grade and is being shunted out of the way by more aggressive colleagues. In either case, the new manager will want to show head office that he is 'doing something', it doesn't much matter whether it is right or wrong; by the time the results show up he will be long gone. After this cycle has been repeated a few times, someone at headquarters will decide that the business is no good and should be disposed of. The truth is that it may have been a perfectly sound business before its owners started trying to find quick solutions to its problems, but by now its staff are shell-shocked and demoralised, its customers bewildered by repeated changes of policy and any manager who was any good will have quit long ago.

It is also possible that, rather than suffering from the corporate equivalent of child abuse, a subsidiary has been enjoying a spoilt and pampered existence under the parental wing which has left it ill-prepared for the cold winds of independence. Being able to rely on a parent as a principal customer or supplier, or as a cheap source of capital, over a period of years, may have simply insulated a business from the market place so effectively that it is unable to stand on its own feet; or it may have been the chairman's personal indulgence or a showpiece business whose value lay more in the image it projected than the profits it made. Such a business, with the silver spoon rudely wrenched from its mouth and forced for the first time to earn its own living, could prove just as bad a buy as one which has been ruthlessly pillaged by its owners.

It may, in the event, prove quite impossible to discover the real reason that a big firm suddenly decides to part with a subsidiary, and the reason may, in any case, be something quite irrelevant, like a boardroom squabble or the need to show shareholders that *something* is being done. What you must do, it is clear from the foregoing, is to try and discover the real, underlying state of the business, discounting those factors which applied when it was part of a much larger business.

Divide and misrule

It is very likely that the buyer with some cash available for a small or medium-sized business will be offered the opportunity to put his nest egg and his energies into an established business where the present owner does not want simply to sell out and retire, but is looking for a new partner, perhaps a potential successor, who can also inject some capital. It may be that the business's expansion is hampered by lack of capital or that the owner has all his capital tied up in the firm and wants to realise some of it by selling shares or taking in a new partner.

Such situations should, however immediately attractive they may look, be approached with a great deal of circumspection. The nub of the matter is, obviously, where control will lie. In too many cases, whatever complimentary things the two parties may say — and mean — about each other, their assumptions will be different. The incoming investor, who is probably looking for scope for his talents just as much as for a home for his money, will assume that once all is signed and sealed he will have at least equal power and an equal voice in the business's affairs. The owner-in-residence, however (who is very likely the founder as well), will assume that once he's got the money he can carry on pretty much as before, making no more than formal acknowledgement of the fact that he now has a partner. It is a tried and tested recipe for disaster.

There are exceptions, but they are best looked upon as proving a well-established rule. It should be added that things are different if the newcomer is content to be a sleeping partner, or is simply looking for a promising investment without any ambitions to get involved in the business — but in that case what we are talking about is really an investment decision, something very different from buying a business which you hope to run as well as own, and one which falls outside the scope of this book. The prudent buyer will have decided at the outset which he wants: a good home for his money with, perhaps, a directorship involving attendance at half a dozen board meetings a year, or a business which is 'his' in fact as well as name, and if his ambition is the latter he will be well advised to settle for nothing less than full control, leaving the sort of opportunity we have been talking about to the individuals and institutions who are looking for sound investments that entail little involvement.

Forced sales

The one circumstance in which you can be quite clear why a business is on the market is the forced sale or the business which has been placed in receivership. Essentially, a business in such a situation has failed under its present owners, which may be the fault of neither the business nor the owner, but puts you, as potential rescuer of a nasty situation, in a strong position. Again, beware of the business up to its neck in financial trouble, which requires just that little bit more cash to see it through to a rosy future. It may be that this is so, but it is a situation where the owner should look to the bank or one of the financial institutions; if he wants a partner who is going to take an active part in the business then you should insist that the price of your help is control of the business after the promised recovery.

Liquidation

A business which has gone into liquidation or receivership has passed out of the hands of the owner into those of the liquidator or receiver. We can, for the purposes of this book, pretty well ignore the business in liquidation. In virtually every case a liquidator will be hoping to sell, not the business as such, but its assets; in other words he will be trying to realise as much as possible of the business's break-up value (see Chapter 4). He will not even be particularly interested in selling the assets in one lump to a single customer, simply because when a business has reached the stage of liquidation, there is unlikely to be any surplus value in the form of goodwill left. Moreover, a liquidator wants to get the whole affair over and done with as quickly and economically as possible, and has no incentive to enter into complex negotiations. Finally, a business that has gone into liquidation has ceased trading, its creditors are out of pocket, and its name is mud.

In the case of a sole trader or partnership, where individuals are personally liable for their business debts, the ultimate price of failure is personal bankruptcy. Clearly, once things have gone that far there is unlikely to be much of a business left. Equally, the prospect of a visit from the bailiffs is a pretty strong incentive for the seller to strike a quick bargain, giving you, as buyer, the whip-hand in negotiations. A word of warning however: in such desperate and unfamiliar circumstances people can be driven to desperate measures and you should take particular care to make sure that the vendor actually owns the assets you are buying. It is likely that in a business which is on the brink of failure the assets will have been pledged as security and you may well regret parting with that thick wodge of tenners when you discover that the office equipment you just bought belongs to a finance company and that the bank has a floating charge on everything else, right down to the office cat.

The failure of a company, however small, is a more elaborate affair, but unless a last minute rescue is effected, the funeral will be in the hands of either the liquidator or the receiver.

Receivership

A receivership is a very different affair. A receiver is normally appointed by a bank or debenture-holder to whom the company owes money. Such a creditor will normally have preference over the company's unsecured creditors and the agreement which gave them that preference, or first call on the company's assets, also gave them the right to appoint a receiver if things began to go wrong. Unlike a liquidator, a receiver is empowered to keep an insolvent company trading if he feels that this is in the best interests of its creditors. In most cases, therefore, he will be aiming to sell the business as a going concern (what will actually be sold is, of course, the assets; no one in their right mind is going to buy the shares of a company in receivership and take on the burden of paying off the creditors in full). He will, however, be under considerable pressure to make a rapid sale, not only because the creditors who appointed him want as much money as is available as fast as possible, but also because they will be aware that the first call on whatever monies there are is the receiver's fees, and the longer he has to spend supervising the business and negotiating with potential purchasers, the more he will charge.

You may find it perfectly possible to strike a quick and advantageous bargain with a receiver, but in one respect you should be extremely cautious. Even though you may have bought all the assets of the company, including the right to use its name, remember that the whole affair will have been painful for at least one group of people, the unsecured creditors, and the fact that you got the assets at a knock-down price means that, when the receiver winds the business up, they will receive even fewer pence in the pound for their debts. Ah well, you may say, it's a hard old world. True enough, but you may need the help and cooperation of some of those creditors if you are to keep the business going. Suppose, for example, that one of the assets you bought was the company's stock which is held in store by a warehouseman who is sitting on an unpaid bill for several hundred pounds. When he gets the news that the best he can hope for is ten pence in the pound his first inclination may be to take 'your' stock and sell it to help make good his loss. Whatever the law may say about it, possession of an asset in such circumstances is nine-tenths of it, and no one, including you, is probably willing to embark on an expensive court action to sort out the rights and wrongs. So if your purchases included goods in the possession of third parties, the benefit of contracts with third parties etc, you must insist that the receiver gets their acceptance in writing of the deal that has been struck and their agreement to release goods, agreement to the assignment of contracts and so forth.

Chapter 3

What is for Sale?
Who is Buying it?

When you decide to buy a business, the first thing to be clear about is what it is that you are buying, exactly. This may not be quite such an elementary matter as it sounds. The simplest kind of business, an individual trading on his own account, a sole trader, cannot be bought and sold as such; what will change hands are the business assets of the individual, for the business itself cannot be separated from its owner. Much the same principle applies, with some complications, to a partnership owned by two or more people; the partnership's business, or a single partner's share in it, cannot be put up for sale. But when a business is organised as a limited company, it has an existence distinct from that of its owners — it pays separate taxes, it can go bankrupt without involving the bankruptcy of its owners, and shares in it can be bought and sold.

Just as the way in which the business which you are buying is organised affects what you actually purchase and the way in which you purchase it, so your options are to some extent limited by how you intend to organise the business once you own it, or, if you are adding it to or amalgamating it with an existing business, by the form which that already takes.

A sole trader

Suppose that you have decided to buy the carpentry business owned by Fred Mortiss, who is a sole trader. All that you can in fact buy are his business assets: his premises, tools and equipment, stocks of wood and other materials. You do not have to buy, nor does he have to sell, all of them. You can, for example, decline to buy that lathe which looks like a survivor from the Industrial Revolution; or he can hang on to his cherished set of hand tools to occupy him in his retirement. If Fred trades under another name, the Cheerful Chippie, say, then you can buy the right to use that name as well. Though if Fred's reputation is that of a bad, bent or bankrupt chippie, you'll obviously be better off finding a new name.

31

But even if you continue to trade under the same name, in the same premises and using the same equipment, the business Fred ran has, in fact, been wound up and you have started a new one. For example, it is up to Fred to settle up with his creditors and to collect all monies owed to him. You will, if you are prudent, have assured yourself, or secured Fred's guarantee, that all the equipment and stock you are buying from him has been bought and paid for and is his to sell, but beyond that you are not concerned with what the business owed or was owed when it belonged to him. The same principle applies to Fred's tax affairs. A sole trader pays income tax on his profits and the business has no tax liability separate from that of its owner; so if the taxman discovers that Fred tried to fiddle his tax return two years ago, or has failed to pay last year's tax, that is a matter between Fred and the Commissioners of Inland Revenue and no concern of yours. Moreover, if Fred has employees whom you do not wish to take on when you acquire the other assets, it is up to him to dismiss them and meet the bill for redundancy pay etc before you take over.

One point to watch out for when evaluating the business of a sole trader is that some assets may not be transferable. For instance, a lease or a contract made with a sole trader is personal to the individual and he may not be able to assign it to a third party. Consider the prosperous dress-making enterprise owned by Constantine Flounce. The prosperity of Flounce Fashions, the rag trade being what it is, may be heavily dependent on Constantine's contract with his cousin Stavros Selvage to deliver two gross of dresses a week, and on the fact that Constantine's premises are rented on extremely favourable terms from his uncle, Aristotle Selvage. Now if the contract or the lease is not freely assignable by Constantine you may find, as the new owner of Flounce Fashions, that Stavros and Aristotle have a much tougher attitude when it comes to doing business outside the family rather than inside it. In other words, Constantine's two main business assets consisted of the benefits of agreements which he was not in a position to sell to you.

Once you have established exactly what a sole trader's assets are, and made your evaluation of them, the actual purchase is a straightforward business, no more complicated in principle than going out and buying the same items piecemeal. It is of no importance to you, except insofar as it affects your negotiations, what Fred Mortiss paid for his workshop, his tools or his stocks, or how much of their purchase price has been written off in his tax returns. Your account with the taxman starts with the price you paid for them. What is important is that the agreement between you and Fred clearly identifies the individual items and the price you paid for them. For you will want to claim capital allowances (if you are a sole trader or partnership) or depreciation (if you are a company) on the fixed assets and you are going to claim the stocks as allowable expenses; even the surplus over cumulative value of the assets, the item for 'goodwill' (see Chapter 5) which you paid, can be written off against future profits for tax purposes. The taxman will, of course, dispute the values if they have been set at ridiculously high levels, but you will make his case a great deal easier for him if you have not distinguished the value attached to individual items.

Partnerships

The business of a partnership, like that of a sole trader, is inseparable from its owners, and neither the partnership as a whole nor the shares of individual partners can be sold or even inherited. Indeed, unless the agreement which governs the conduct of a partnership provides otherwise, a partnership is automatically dissolved by the death, retirement or insolvency of a partner.

Let us suppose that the carpentry business you are interested in is a partnership between Fred Mortiss and his friend Tom Tenon. Now if both Fred and Tom want to sell, you are in just the same position as you were with Fred as sole trader. You can buy the assets, but not the business itself, of Mortiss and Tenon; again, the creditors and debtors and the tax affairs of previous business remain entirely the business of Fred and Tom.

But what is the position if, while Fred wants to sell out, Tom wants to continue the business with a new partner? You cannot simply buy Fred's share; what has to happen, on paper at least, is that the partnership of Mortiss and Tenon is dissolved and its assets sold to the new partnership between Tom and yourself. It will certainly be more convenient if this takes place at the end of an accounting period, for the creditors, debtors and tax liabilities of the old partnership must be kept separate from those of the new one. The tax owed by the partnership of Mortiss and Tenon will, for example, depend in part upon Fred's personal circumstances (the allowances he is entitled to etc) whereas that owed by the new business will depend upon your own circumstances. This is because, though the accounts of a partnership set out the profit it has made as a whole, the tax due is calculated separately on each partner's share (though, it should be added, the total tax due is a debt of the partnership rather than the individual partners).

Before agreeing to become Tom's new partner you must also be quite clear about the basis of the arrangement. Unless the partnership agreement provides otherwise, for instance, the law assumes that control, and profit, are divided equally between partners, regardless of the financial stakes held by them. And remember, Tom is not leaving his money in the business, he is taking it out of one business and putting it into another, and your new partnership agreement must clearly state the amounts of capital which both of you are putting up.

Exactly the same considerations arise if, rather than taking the place of an existing partner, you are joining an existing partnership. Technically, in most cases the result is a new partnership. This is particularly important if you are, for instance, injecting new funds into a partnership which is in trouble. Let us say that you have become interested in joining the rather moribund estate agency owned by Michael Modcon and Ephraim Gazumper, and that you have £10,000 to spare to revivify the business. If you simply make a loan to the business all well and good — provided you trust Michael and Ephraim — but if you invest the money in the partnership then it is no longer a matter of your owning £10,000 and Michael and Ephraim each owning half of some rather scruffy offices valued, on paper, at £20,000. You now own a third of the offices and Michael and Ephraim each own a third of the £10,000 in the partnership's bank account. Moreover, if your two new partners continue to make a mess of the business, or try to conceal their profits from the taxman, then you could, in the last resort, find yourself liable for, not one-third, but all the losses or the tax bill.

Buying the assets of a partnership *in toto* is, therefore, no more complicated in principle than buying those of a sole trader — though it should be noted that in practice it may be considerably more so, since all the partners will have to agree on the terms of the sale and it is unlikely that one of them will have the power to negotiate for the partnership as a whole on such a fundamental issue. Buying into an existing partnership, in contrast, is likely to be a complicated affair and one fraught with imponderables of personality as well as business.

If you, the purchaser, are acting on behalf of a partnership the same factors operate. Simply buying assets is relatively straightforward, providing that you can persuade your partners to agree and stick to a definite set of limits to your freedom to negotiate on price and conditions of sale. But if the purchase of a business involves taking on one or more new partners and merging their interests with your existing ones, you are in effect creating a new business, possibly with a new and different balance of power between the individuals involved and, however great the disparity in size between the two businesses, your new partners are in effect buying a share in your business in the same way as you are buying a share in theirs.

Limited companies

Buying a publicly quoted company, or making a takeover bid in the stock market, is clearly outside the scope of this book. But the purchase of even the smallest private company is in essence a more complicated affair than buying the assets of a sole trader or partnership.

You can avoid the complications by purchasing the assets rather than the company; indeed the choice between these two possible alternatives is the first and fundamental one whenever the question of buying a company arises. Simply buying the assets puts you in exactly the same position, and subject to the same considerations, as buying the assets of a sole trader or partnership — it has the virtues of simplicity, speed and convenience but, nonetheless, it may not always be the right course.

The key to understanding the issues involved is that a company has an existence in law quite separate and distinct from that of its owners — after all, the ownership of a public company changes to some degree each time a block of its shares is traded on the floor of the Stock Exchange without affecting the day-to-day running of the company at all. So when ownership, or even a controlling share, of a company changes hands, the new owner or controlling shareholder inherits a business which has creditors, debtors, tax liabilities and contractual benefits and obligations which are quite separate from those of its old owners or its new ones. This can bring advantages and disadvantages. For example, leases or contracts entered into by the company will continue to be valid no matter who owns the business. In the same way, though, the company's obligations under its contracts of employment with its work force are not invalidated by a change of ownership, and if there are to be redundancies, for example, the company will have to foot the bill.

The fact that a company has a separate legal existence means that it is normally sold as a going concern and, in addition to evaluating the assets such as property, equipment and stock, a purchaser will have to look closely at its debtors and creditors. Are there potentially bad debts concealed in the debtors figure? Have all the creditors been held at bay for the last six months and will they descend in a ravenous mob the moment a new owner takes over? Even more seriously, are the figures for both groups complete and up to date? Are there potential or outstanding claims against the company for, say, negligence or defective goods? These are matters on which you, as a purchaser, will want checks made by your accountants and lawyers and as watertight a warranty from the vendor as your solicitor can construct.

The same applies to the company's relationship with the taxman. If, under the previous owners, the company paid less tax than it should, then the Inland Revenue will, when it discovers the underpayment, look to the company, not its previous owners, to pay up. The possibility of a tax liability arising in respect of past years is a contingency which the purchaser will want to provide against by checks and by warranties from the vendors.

A further complication, possibly advantageous, arises from the fact that companies paying *corporation tax*, unlike individuals paying income tax (except in very limited circumstances), can set a loss made in one year against a profit made in a later year and thus reduce their tax bill. If, for instance, you become the owner of a company which lost £500 last year and £750 the year before, then, all other things being equal, it can make a profit of up to £1250 in this year without incurring any liability for corporation tax. This factor can make a company with a record of losses more attractive than it might appear at first glance. But, because of the readiness with which such tax losses could be abused, the use that can be made of them is strictly regulated. In general, any profit which is to be set against the loss must derive from the same trade, so it is no use buying a chemist's shop with a vast accumulated loss in the hope of setting that loss against the profits you will make when you transform it into an off-licence. Again, the profit to be offset must be the result of trading by the same enterprise as the one that made the loss, so you would be on dodgy ground even if you bought the loss-making chemist and turned it into a subsidiary of your profitable chemist shop in the hope of setting its past losses against your present profit. The one case when a tax loss is undoubtedly attractive is where it is clearly the result of a business, which you are sure you can run profitably in the future, being badly run in the past; provided you do not change the nature of the business or merge it with other undertakings you are perfectly entitled to have the benefit of the established tax loss.

Tax considerations are not the only ones that arise if both the business that is purchased and the purchaser are companies. To start with, a company has the option of buying another company (or indeed the assets of any other business) in exchange for an issue of its own shares rather than for cash. In effect, a company doing this is saying to the seller, 'In exchange for ownership of, or control over, your business assets, I will give you shares in the larger business which they will now form part of'. In theory this seems an attractive option for the buyer. Who, after all, would not prefer to part with a few slips of printed paper in the shape of share certificates rather than with hard won cash? The snag is that by issuing more shares in his own company the purchaser is reducing his own share in it, and also perhaps a degree of his control. There can be an element of self-deception involved, as many of the takeover enthusiasts of the sixties and seventies discovered.

Take the case of Gerry Gogetter of Gogo Toys Ltd. He started Gogo, and owned 900 of the original 1000 shares in it (his wife, Emma Gogetter, owned the other 100). But Gerry soon got impatient with the slow business of building up a small company and decided to buy a rival company, Sleepyhead Playthings, in exchange for shares in Gogo. Since he wasn't actually parting with any cash, Gerry was generous and issued 500 shares in the new, larger Gogo to the Sleepyhead share-holders. But while the acquisition of Sleepyhead may have made Gogo 50 per cent larger, even after the improvements Gerry made, it only increased the profits by 25 per cent, and instead of getting 100 per cent of these profits, the Gogetter family was now only entitled to 66 per cent of them. In effect, the purchase of Sleepyhead had resulted in Gerry giving away quite a chunk of the profit which Gogo had been earning before the takeover. Moreover, the next time he wanted to take over a company by issuing shares, it wouldn't be so easy, for the shares in the enlarged Gogo would obviously be less attractive than those of the old firm.

It can be seen that the issuing of new shares to acquire a company can be a double-edged weapon and one that can easily be blunted with repeated use. Its fundamental drawback is that it inevitably dilutes your ownership, and control, of your business.

When you consider buying a company, another possibility is that of buying some, rather than all, of the shares. The crucial point is, naturally, who has control of the business. For all day-to-day purposes, the ownership of 51 per cent of the shares gives control; with 76 per cent of the shares comes absolute control within the limits of the law — the percentages refer only to voting shares if there are two or more classes of share, some of which do not have the benefit of voting.

In practice, the partial acquisition of a small private company is uncommon, simply because of this question of control. It is attractive to neither buyer nor seller to have an investment in a company over which they can exercise no control. Nonetheless, the option exists, and can be used, for example, to spread the process of acquisition over time, with the purchaser gradually acquiring a preponderance of shares and control as a result of a series of transactions. It has the advantage over the issuing of new shares in a merged business that the purchaser retains ownership and control of the original undertaking, and it has the obvious disadvantage that the buyer's freedom to combine the two businesses or to merge one into the other may be limited.

Groups and consolidated accounts

If you are the controlling shareholder in company A and wish to expand your activities by the acquisition of company B, there are three basic ways you can go about it. Company B, or a controlling proportion of its shares, can be purchased by company A, either for cash or by means of an issue of shares as described above. Or, as explained earlier, company A can simply buy the assets of company B. And finally, you can purchase company B as an individual. The choice between these two methods may have a profound influence on how the businesses are run and, in particular, on how their accounts are prepared and their profits taxed.

If you hold controlling interests in the two companies separately, then as far as the rest of the world is concerned they have nothing to do with each other. If you go the other way about it, and your existing company buys more than 50 per cent of the ordinary shares of the other one, or puts itself in a position to control the membership of its board of directors, then you have created a 'group' and you are legally obliged to produce consolidated accounts which show the *net* profits and worth of the two businesses combined, less any share of them which may continue to belong to other, minority, shareholders.

To come back to Gerry Gogetter of Gogo Toys and his takeover of Sleepyhead Playthings, let us suppose that Gogo has a balance sheet worth £40,000 and annual profits of £10,000, whereas Sleepyhead had assets of £20,000 and losses of £2000 a year. The price the Sleepyhead shareholders set was £20,000 (we will look at what happens when the price paid for a company is greater or smaller than its balance sheet value in Chapter 4). If Gerry went out and personally raised the £20,000, he would own two quite separate companies, and if he had to make good the £2000 loss each year in order to keep Sleepyhead going he would have to draw on the (taxed) profits of Gogo to do so. But Gogo would continue to be a successful business in its own right and only Gerry's personal fortunes would be affected by Sleepyhead's affairs; and if things got so bad at Sleepyhead that it had to go into liquidation, this could be done without affecting the fortunes of Gogo.

If Gogo simply bought the assets of Sleepyhead, then the two businesses would to all intents and purposes have become one and the profits made by the Gogo part of it would offset the losses made by the Sleepyhead bit. But the Gogo accounts would soon reveal the fact that buying Sleepyhead's assets had been an error, and if the deal pushed the business down the slippery slope it would not be possible to separate the profitable, Gogo, bits from the unprofitable, Sleepyhead, ones.

The situation that arises if Gogo buys the share capital, rather than merely the assets, of Sleepyhead is more complicated. Gogo now becomes a holding company in that it owns a controlling interest in Sleepyhead, and the two combined form a group. Each company continues to trade and produce accounts independently. If they combine or share aspects of their businesses then they must pay each other for work done or goods exchanged. And if Sleepyhead continues to decline it can go into liquidation without dragging Gogo down with it. In other words, the relationship between the two companies continues, in law, to be an arm's-length one. But, as a holding company, Gogo will have to produce consolidated accounts which will show not only the profit it makes from its own operations but also the loss it incurs as a shareholder in Sleepyhead. The advantage of this is that Gogo will at least save the corporation tax payable on its own profits to the extent that they are offset by Sleepyhead's current losses (the matter of Sleepyhead's previous losses is more difficult; see page 37); the disadvantage is that the consolidated accounts will reveal to the world, and to shareholders and bankers in particular, the extent to which Gogo's fortunes have suffered as a result of its involvement with Sleepyhead.

Buying a franchise

The franchise is a relatively modern — and very ingenious — invention which, though in practice similar to any small business, has legal and financial implications which distinguish it from other businesses, whether it takes the form of a sole trader, partnership or limited company. Franchising had its origins in America during the last century, where centralised distribution was not the most effective way of selling a product over a vast territory.

Although the term 'franchise' now covers a whole range of arrangements (such as the use of a celebrity name to endorse a product), the readers of this book will be most interested in 'business format franchising'. Basically, if you are considering purchasing a franchise business, you will be acquiring a licence to sell products or services associated with the franchisor's name (and trademark) within a certain geographical area in return for a royalty or fee based on your turnover or profit. Fast food chains, such as Kentucky Fried Chicken, are perhaps the most common examples of franchises in action. Although by law you will own the business, the franchisor provides an entire 'blueprint' for the operation of the business which may include the decor of the premises, how the product is to be sold, and 'secret recipes' in its manufacture, employees' dress, location etc, as well as, say, book-keeping methods. In addition, the franchisor will advertise the franchised product in general and often supplies funds for promotion of a specific franchisee; financial advice (such as how to raise funds) and market research (such as the favourability of a certain location) are part of the entire package.

Advantages of franchising

The advantages of buying a franchise are obvious. For one thing, it is usually a much quicker way of purchasing and managing a small business and, even though you will be sharing your profits with the franchisor, the fame of his trademark and the professional quality of his management and advertising will protect you from some of the risks normally borne by independent enterprises. You will be running a business which has been tried and tested and your budgeting and accounts will be done according to a formula. And, finally, with the big name of the franchisor backing you, you may find it much easier to raise the capital to purchase the franchise.

Franchising drawbacks

The drawbacks to owning a franchise are less obvious but should be seriously considered if you are contemplating such a purchase. The most important disadvantage is lack of flexibility once the shop or restaurant is actually in business. Suppose, for instance, that you buy a franchise from the huge fast food chain, 'Sink or Swim', which specialises in fish and chips. You, with their advice and approval, locate your Sink or Swim shop in a busy university town full of hungry students eager for fish and chips. You are a good manager and a keen entrepreneur and you manage to turn your franchised shop into a money-making success within a matter of months; this established, you begin to turn your mind to even better ways of drawing in more students. You note that many of them ask if you sell yoghurt and you realise it would be a splendid addition to your dairy shelf. But Sink or Swim headquarters tell you that yoghurt does 'not fit in with the corporate image', whereas this year's 'special' product happens to be tartare sauce which you, and your customers, find particularly revolting. Remember that this inflexibility applies right across the board even to the way you keep your books, which could prove frustrating if you are the type of small businessman who relishes innovation and risk.

There are, in principle, two ways in which you can buy a franchise. One is to go directly to the franchisor; the other is to purchase it from a franchisee who has already set up trade — although he may have to ask the franchisor's permission to sell. In any case, you will probably obtain some advice and help from the franchisor in getting the finance you need for the purchase.

The whole field of franchises is full of complications and snags, which space considerations do not allow this book to go into. It is certainly an area in which to seek specialised advice and the best way to begin might be by reading *Taking up a Franchise* by Godfrey Golzen and Colin Barrow.

Management buy-outs

One other possibility which has become fashionable in recent years is the so-called 'management buy-out'. This normally occurs in the case of fairly large businesses, or subsidiaries of large businesses, since it involves the professional management of an enterprise buying it from its owners. Such buy-outs will normally involve raising capital from institutional sources (see Chapter 7) on the premise that the executives' experience and expertise will enable them to dramatically improve the performance of the business. As you will realise, should you find yourself in a position to buy out the business for which you work, far and away your strongest card is the fact that you already know the business inside out, you have access to all the facts and figures and you have, presumably, some very clear ideas about what is currently wrong with it and how it should be put right.

Chapter 4

Judging the Track Record

Whatever the nature of the business you are planning to buy, and however you intend to go about arranging the purchase, the one hard piece of evidence you have by which to measure both its present value and its future prospects is the record of past performance in the shape of the accounts.

A sole trader is under no legal compulsion to keep accounts at all; he only needs to do so insofar as he has to satisfy the tax inspector that he has fully and truly declared the income from his business. But in the absence of proper accounts, whatever a trader tells you about his past success and profits must clearly be taken with the most generous pinch of salt. A partnership, on the other hand, has a legal obligation to keep accounts, though not to have them audited. A company not only has to keep accounts and employ auditors to inspect them, but also has to file them at Companies House where they are open to public inspection.

As a prospective purchaser, you clearly have a right to see past accounts; in the case of sole traders and partnerships, however, the vendor has no obligation to show you the balance sheet. Since you are, as we have seen in Chapter 3, buying the assets of the business rather than the business itself, the information in the balance sheet — the value the vendor places on those assets, the amount of money he invested to acquire or build up the business, the monies owed to or by him and the way in which ownership is divided — is irrelevant to you and might strengthen your hand against his in negotiation. But you may view a refusal to let you see the balance sheet as evidence that, on one or more of these counts, the vendor has something to hide.

Assuming that you are shown a full set of accounts — and to form a worthwhile picture these will have to cover a period of at least three years, ending with those for the last complete financial year of the business — they should be considered under the four headings they will normally be divided into:

Trading Account
Profit and Loss Account
Balance Sheet
Statement showing the Sources and Application of Funds.

You must study any notes which the accountants or auditors have attached which will explain the policies followed on matters like depreciation and also provide explanations of unusual or complicated items.

The trading account

Examples of trading accounts are shown on pages 49-51.

Turnover

The first item in the trading account of any business will be the total of its sales for the year — its turnover. Comparing the figures for different years is obviously a crude guide to whether or not the business is growing, and if so, how fast. You must, of course, allow for inflation. If the sales turnover of a business has risen by 10 per cent a year while the price of the goods which it sells has risen by 11 per cent a year it has, in real terms, been shrinking, in that it has sold fewer goods each year.

Cost of sales

The next item will be the cost of sales (which may, according to the kind of business concerned, be variously described as 'purchases', 'production costs', or whatever). This figure will, however it is labelled or sub-divided, include the cost of raw materials or finished goods together with the costs of freight or delivery on them, and, in a manufacturing business, the costs of making the raw materials into saleable goods, ie labour, energy etc.

In the case of a shop, the figure is a straightforward one: it is simply the total bill for goods purchased during the year plus any delivery charges involved. But in other businesses, especially those involved in a manufacturing process, the cost of sales may be the result of extremely complex and crucial calculations and you will certainly want to see the detailed figures on which it is based. These may take the form of a separate manufacturing account which breaks down the costs of the manufacturing process into such items as materials, labour, energy, property costs (rent and rates), the depreciation of machinery etc. These

individual figures may well be the key to reaching a judgement about how efficiently the business has been run and what improvements can be made. They will reveal, for instance, whether wages have been rising faster than the value of goods which the work force produces, or whether the business premises are cheap or costly and thus, perhaps, what would be lost or gained by moving it to a new location.

Stock

The next entries in the trading account will deal with stock. In some instances, a greengrocer or a fishmonger, say, stock is a fairly minor item limited to the value of goods in a freezer cabinet or a cold room; but in others the way in which it is treated may be quite crucial. In all cases the principle is the same: the opening stock held by the business at the beginning of the accounting period must be added to the cost of sales at whatever figure it was valued in the previous set of accounts (where it was, of course, the closing stock) and the closing stock for the period must be deducted. For a business like a retailer stock consists simply of the unsold goods on the shelves and in the stockroom; but a manufacturer may hold raw materials and partially finished goods as well as items ready for sale. His stock will therefore be broken down into materials (which may be further categorised under different headings), work in progress and finished goods.

The notes to the accounts will tell you on what basis stocks have been valued, the commonest ones being defined as 'the lower of cost or net realisable value' and 'replacement cost'. Cost means what the business paid for them in terms of a bill from a supplier and/or manufacturing work done. Net realisable value is what the business reckons it can sell them for, less the costs of selling them. It is clearly misleading to say that those 10,000 mousetraps in the warehouse can be sold for a pound apiece if you do not deduct the £5000-worth of advertising that is going to be necessary to shift them; though if they only cost 25p each to make, the total cost of £2500 is lower than the net realisable value so the lower, 'cost' figure is a fair one. 'Replacement value' means what it says and is accurate insofar as it gives the cost of getting new stock when the old is sold, but misleading in that, inflation being a fact of life, the replacement value may well be greater than the cost.

The difficulty with a business that carries heavy stocks is that the valuation is, in the end, a matter of judgement. Auditors will obviously not allow a furniture shop, say, to continue to value its stock of 20 chromium plated sofas at cost when the last one was sold ten years ago, but few cases are as clear cut as that. The danger for the buyer is, of course, that stocks have been overvalued. This not only means that he may pay more for them than they are worth, but also that the previous profit record has been distorted.

You can only judge the value of the stocks you are actually buying by looking at the stock itself and comparing the value attached to materials with their current market price or the value of finished goods with the sales records for that particular item. But a year by year comparison of the figures for closing stocks will show whether there has been a build-up, either of stocks themselves or in the value attached to them. The one thing you should watch out for, and if necessary enquire into in detail, is whether, in a business which carries heavy stocks (especially if they are of a kind likely to become out of date or are subject to changes in fashion or demand) there has been any change in the assumptions made when valuing stock. You are obviously being misled if the very handsome profit the business made last year is due to its failure to write off the value of a warehouse full of unsaleable goods; you are, perhaps less obviously, being misled if its sudden recovery from bad losses two years ago is due to the fact that a large chunk of stock was written off, giving rise to the loss, and has since been sold at a handsome, paper, profit. The actual basis of valuation used, provided it has been consistently applied to a consistent level of stocks over a number of years, doesn't matter (though it is important when it comes to evaluating the stock you are actually buying, as we shall see in Chapter 5). For, given a steady level of business, the effects of any particular method balance themselves out over time. Thus a business which has always written off unsold stock at the end of each year, though it in fact sells it during the next year, makes a high paper profit from the sale of worthless stock but balances that by writing off a new lot of stock at the year's end. In contrast, a business which carries a lot of stock forward from year to year at cost will make less profit on the sale of that stock but will have a new lot of stock to include in its next set of accounts at the same, cost, value. The problem arises with businesses that have not applied consistent criteria to valuing their stock.

By comparing the figure for opening stock with the turnover for the year you get the business's rate of stock turn, a ratio which is a vital criterion of well-being. It will vary enormously with the nature of the business: a supermarket may work on the basis that it turns over the stock on its shelves once a fortnight whereas an antique shop, say, may be happy if it does so once a year. So there are no absolute standards to judge by; it is up to you to discover, if you do not already know, the average rate for the trade concerned. The importance of a good rate of stock turn should be clear. A business which carries £10,000-worth of stock and sells £100,000-worth of goods a year is, providing the profit margin is the same, doing twice as well as a competitor with the same stock level but annual sales of only £50,000 — the former has a rate of stock turn of ten whereas the latter is struggling along at five.

Gross profit

After deducting the cost of sales from the turnover and making the necessary allowances for stock, you are left with the figure at the foot of the trading account: the gross profit. The basic point to establish is whether this figure, as a percentage of the turnover, is rising or falling. A falling gross profit margin indicates a business whose costs of sales have been rising while its sales were falling, or static or, at best, one in which costs of sales have been outpacing sales. A rising margin suggests improving efficiency, with income from sales increasing faster than the cost of those sales.

Trading account: Summary

To see the sort of information that can be derived from the trading account, and how it may vary from business to business, it will be worthwhile looking at some examples. In each case we shall be taking two years together, for the purposes of comparison.

To start with, we'll look at a retailer with a quick turnover of stock and, therefore, a stock value which is comparatively low in proportion to turnover — a delicatessen, perhaps.

	Year One		Year Two	
	£	£	£	£
Sales	70,000		80,000	
Cost of Sales				
Purchases		50,000		60,000
Freight		1,200		1,800
		51,200		61,800
Opening Stock*		4,000		4,500
		54,200		66,300
Less Closing Stock		4,500		5,000
	49,700		61,300	
Gross Profit	20,300		18,700	

* valued at cost

The basic figures you can calculate from this are: turnover
has gone up from £70,000 to £80,000, an increase of just over
14 per cent, which looks good. The rate of stock turn, 17.5
times in year one and 17.7 in year two, seems steady.

The gross profit, however, has actually fallen in both absolute
and percentage terms. It is down from over 28 per cent to under
23 per cent of turnover. It does not take a business genius to see
that the problem lies in the steep rise in the cost of goods
purchased, from £50,000 to £60,000, a rise of 20 per cent,
and it is also clear that this is not due to having heavy stocks
at the end of year two, for the stock is valued at cost and the
difference between opening stock and closing stock in year two
is exactly the same as in year one, £500. So it looks as if the
margin the shop is working on has shrunk dramatically. Perhaps
they have switched to goods where the wholesaler's discount is
smaller, or perhaps they have been cutting their prices; either
way it is a worrying trend, and one which you will want a
very full explanation of. While you are at it, do not skip over
that increase in freight costs; an extra £600 may seem fairly
negligible in a business turning over £80,000 a year, but in a
business with a gross profit of under £19,000 it represents
over 3 per cent of the profit — maybe the difference between
a week in Blackpool and a package tour in Ibiza next year.
It is worth finding out why it has suddenly jumped up like that
and whether it can be made to go down again.

Next, let us take a very different kind of business, a timber merchant, for example, who has a great deal of money tied up in stocks.

	Year One		Year Two	
	£	£	£	£
Sales	180,000		185,000	
Cost of Sales				
Purchases		100,000		90,000
Freight inwards		10,000		9,000
		110,000		99,000
Opening Stock*		50,000		55,000
		160,000		154,000
Less Closing Stock*		55,000		64,000
		105,000		90,000
Gross Profit	75,000		95,000	

* valued at replacement cost

Wow, you may say, the turnover has barely increased (under 3 per cent), but the gross profit has gone up from about 41 per cent to over 51 per cent — clever chap. Well, perhaps not. The rate of stock turn has gone down from 3.6 to 3.35, quite a serious drop when the stock represents such a large amount of capital tied up; moreover, as the closing stock at the end of year two shows, this situation looks as if it is getting worse rather than better. Of the £20,000 increase in gross profit, no less than £9000 is represented by an increase in stock values, and, since the turnover and the rate of stock turn is falling it is unlikely that that increased stock is going to be translated into sales very rapidly. In fact, since the stock is valued at replacement cost, it is quite likely that the increased stock value represents a revaluation of stocks that have been held in the yard for two years or more. Indeed, since purchases have fallen it is scarcely likely that they are new stocks. It would be as well to check very carefully indeed before finding yourself the proud owner of a yard full of timber which nobody wants to buy. The suspicion must be that the present owner's purchases, and therefore sales, are falling because all his available cash is tied up in stock which, while its value may increase every year on paper, sells very slowly indeed.

Matters become more complicated, naturally, in manufacturing businesses. To demonstrate this, look at the trading account of something like a small precision engineering firm.

	Year One		Year Two	
	£	£	£	£
Sales	300,000		345,000	
Cost of Sales				
Materials		45,000		60,000
Manufacturing		160,000		203,000
		205,000		263,000
Opening Stock*				
Materials		5,000		6,000
Work in Progress		10,000		12,000
Finished Goods		10,000		12,000
		230,000		293,000
Less Closing Stock				
Materials		6,000		10,000
Work in Progress		12,000		23,000
Finished Goods		12,000		20,000
		30,000		53,000
		200,000		240,000
Gross Profit	100,000		105,000	

* at lower of cost or net realisable value

Turnover seems to have risen quite nicely by £45,000 or 15 per cent, but the gross profit figure has risen by only 5 per cent. Stock turn has stayed reasonably steady, though the increase in stock values at the end of year two looks worrying, on the face of it. To find the roots of the problem in year two, though, it is necessary to look at the two figures that have increased out of all proportion to the turnover: materials and manufacturing costs. The former has risen by no less than 51 per cent and the latter by well over 20 per cent. For the sake of non-engineers, imagine that the factory is making something very simple like that perennial product, widgets.

Turning to the manufacturing account you find that the materials that go into a widget cost about £1. If you then look at the closing stock figures for year two you find that though the increase in purchases of materials was dramatic, it is partially balanced by the increased stocks of materials, work in progress and completed widgets. Provided that the market for widgets is holding up well this may not be a problem — it may reflect no more than the fact that the firm got a whacking great order for widgets just before the end of the year and had to stock up with materials. On the other hand, the manufacturing accounts show that the labour costs of making a widget have increased by 25p, from £0.90 to £1.15, and the firm's inability to increase its prices to compensate for this accounts for most of the reduction in the gross profit percentage (and also for the remainder of the increase in stock value). All may yet be well in the coming year if there is scope for increasing the price of the widgets already in stock, in progress and to be made out of the stock materials; if not things could get sticky for the new owner since, if he buys the stocks at valuation, he is buying stocks which have a reduced profit margin built into them.

Finally, if all this arithmetic has left you battered and bewildered, it is worth pointing out that in many businesses the trading account is very simple, or even non-existent. An architect's business, or an estate agency for example, has no goods or materials to purchase, no stocks to value; in such cases the gross profit is essentially the same as the turnover.

The profit and loss account

The profit and loss account (P&L for short) starts with the gross profit figure from the trading account and deducts from it all the other costs of the business in order to arrive at the net, pre-tax, profit. In some cases there may also be additional items of income which show up in the profit and loss account; these will be items which come from peripheral or subsidiary aspects of the business and are not part of its mainstream trading. For example, a manufacturing firm which lets out a part of its premises to another company will show the rent received under 'other income' or some such heading in the P&L.

But most of the P&L will be concerned with costs, often loosely described as overheads, which are not directly related to the purchase or manufacture of the business's stock in trade. In most cases these can be divided into four main categories:

Administrative costs
Selling costs
Financial charges (ie, interest paid)
Depreciation.

The relative importance of the different categories, and of

individual items within them, will naturally vary enormously from one kind of business to another. A firm which keeps half a dozen reps on the road will have large figures for travelling expenses but may have a comparatively modest phone bill, whereas in one that does most of its selling by mail the largest selling cost may be postage.

The essential thing is not to assess the figures by some absolute standard, but to compare one year with another and try and identify the trends. Have advertising costs risen out of proportion to the increase in sales? Is the office rent or rates bill mounting too fast? Is the sales force or the distribution system costing too much?

Administrative costs
Administrative costs, which usually include all the items that cannot be fitted in elsewhere (like the chairman's expense account or the office cleaning service), are usually where you will be able to detect the signs of a business that has become wasteful or self-indulgent. Here you will normally find the figure for wages and salaries (other than those of production staff), entertainment, travel etc. By looking at the figure for directors' remuneration, in conjunction with the notes giving the salary ranges of directors which are a legal requirement in company accounts, you should be able to calculate what the owners are taking out of the business by way of salaries; with a small business the totals for travel, entertainment and motor expenses may well enable you to make a guess at the level of benefits in kind which they are drawing. You will then be able to judge whether, if your needs are less, you can cut costs in this area or, if you hope for a more elaborate business life-style, whether you will be able to afford it.

Selling costs
Selling costs (which usually include distribution costs) greatly depend on the kind of business concerned, but again, the thing to look for is the trend over two or three years and the relationship between the costs and the sales that result from them.

Financial charges
In the case of a sole trader or a partnership, when you may not get a sight of the balance sheet, the financial charges (the interest paid to the bank or other lenders) will still enable you

to make a fairly accurate estimate of how the present owners have 'geared' the business, ie what the balance is between the owner's funds and borrowed money. In such cases, of course, this is of only indirect interest to you, for you will be buying the assets rather than the business and may have quite different plans for financing it in the future. But if you know, even roughly, how much money the present owner has borrowed for the business you will be able to judge your negotiating position that much more accurately. If it is clear that the borrowings run to five figures, for example, it is a reasonable guess that your four-figure offer is not going to be very attractive, for it will not provide enough money for the vendor to pay off his bank borrowings, let alone give him anything over to put in his pocket.

The profit and loss account will also reveal any bad debts the business has had to write off and, perhaps more importantly from the purchaser's point of view, the overall level of bad debts over a period of years. A sole trader and a partnership can only write off bad debts if they are able to identify each individual debt and satisfy the taxman that they are indeed unlikely to be able to collect it. A company, on the other hand, may establish the principle of making an allowance for bad debts in its P&L which reflects past experience. If a bad debt has proved to be collectable in time, then the amount written off will, of course, have to be written back in the next set of accounts.

Depreciation

A sole trader or a partnership cannot charge depreciation against their profit for tax, though they can of course do so for their own purpose. As far as the taxman is concerned, they deduct from their profits 'capital allowances', which amount to much the same thing. The depreciation item in the P&L refers to the depreciation of the business's fixed assets (stock depreciation has, as we have seen, already been taken care of in the trading account, and in a manufacturing business the depreciations of production machinery may also have been included in the cost of sales).

There are three possible methods of calculating depreciation, and the notes to the accounts will tell you which has been employed. The *straight line* method simply takes the initial cost of the item and reduces it in equal stages over its anticipated life. Thus, the depreciation on a machine costing £1000 and expected to last for ten years will be £100 per year. The *reducing balance* method works by deducting a set percentage, but the percentage applies to the residual value not the cost. Thus the depreciation on the £1000 machine, assuming that it has been decided to depreciate at the rate of 10 per cent per year, will be £100 in the first year, but in year two it will be 10 per cent of the residual value of £900, or £90, and in year three 10 per cent of £810, or £81. Finally, there is the *revaluation method*, usually applied to smaller items where keeping track of original cost and residual value would be too elaborate a procedure. The assets are valued each year and the depreciation is simply the difference between the valuation at the beginning of the period plus purchases made during it and the valuation at the end of it.

Net profit

The bottom line of the profit and loss account is, of course, the net profit. Though this is the ultimate criterion of the success and, therefore, the worth of the business, it must be borne in mind that in many small businesses the net profit figure will have been manipulated, within the law, to make the best of the owner's tax position. At the simplest level, for example, a sole trader will almost certainly have paid his wife a salary up to the current maximum of the *wife's earned income allowance*. While he will have had to justify this by demonstrating that his wife does help in the business, the actual sum is likely to be fixed by the desire to take advantage of the tax concession rather than by the amount of work involved. It may well be that the wife has been working her fingers to the bone day in and day out and if he had to hire someone to do her work he would have to pay them five or six times as much; equally, it is perfectly possible that her contribution to the business was limited to answering the phone while her husband was out at the pub.

In the same way, a sole trader or a partnership may well have gone as far as the tax inspector would allow in charging household expenses like electricity, telephone, rates etc to the business. There is nothing reprehensible about this, but it is a factor you must take into account in assessing the real profitability of the business. The brand new Mercedes, and the petrol it consumes, or the high rates bill in a fashionable part of town, may well reflect the owner's tastes and interests rather than the real, irreducible costs of running the business.

In most cases, provided that he has not actually strayed over the legal borderlines, the vendor will probably be only too happy to give you information on this aspect of his business: after all, it is very much in his interest to persuade you that his profits have been understated.

The same complications can arise in company accounts. The managing director and owner of a small company will almost certainly prefer to take as much of his profit as he can out of the business in the form of travel, entertainment, etc rather than as salary or dividends which are taxable. Thus his expensive selling trip to Hong Kong may not have been a total necessity, and his highly paid secretary may be just as involved in organising his social life as in meeting his business needs.

Disentangling this sort of factor from the accounts can be very difficult. In the case of a company the accounts will include, as already mentioned, a statement showing the salary ranges of the directors who, in the case of a small business are likely to be, or at least to include, the owners. You will also be able to make some judgements about the level of travelling, entertainment and motoring expenses and in the course of visiting the business and meeting the vendor you will probably be able to get a reasonably accurate sense of his life-style and how much of it is paid for by the business. But do not get carried away, or be persuaded that profits could be vastly increased by a less spendthrift proprietor. You too will probably want to take advantage of the tax concessions that exist, and the joy of owning an amazingly profitable business is certainly diminished if you have to ride ten miles to work on a bike and eat sandwiches for lunch every day to make sure profits stay up.

Profit and loss account: Summary

Analysing any P&L is more a matter of comparisons than absolutes; what is important are the trends in each category over the years and the comparison with similar costs in comparable businesses. The usual method employed is to take each major category and express it as a percentage of the turnover or the gross profit. Suppose, for example, that you take the rent and rates total for each year and compare it with the turnover. Let us say the figures look like this:

	Year One £	Year Two £	Year Three £
Turnover	60,000	65,000	70,000
Rent and Rates	5,000	5,800	6,500
Percentage	8.3	9.0	9.3

The absolute increases, £800 and £700, may not be frightening in themselves but the trend is worrying and, if a similar trend was revealed in, say, the sales costs of a mail order business or the wages bill of an office it could be very serious indeed.

When comparing the level of costs with those in other businesses, a process that will, if it is to be useful, again involve expressing them as a percentage of turnover or gross profit, it is particularly important to make sure that you are comparing like with like. Most trades have some simple rules of thumb, such as advertising should run at about 7 per cent of sales or the going rate for sales and distribution costs is 20 per cent of turnover, and such figures can provide a useful yardstick. But those who fling them about at conferences or in periodicals are often rather vague about how they are defined, a difficulty that is compounded by the fact that accountants may choose somewhat arbitrarily the categories into which costs are broken down. For example, it is perfectly possible that in the case of two comparable companies, both of which employ travelling representatives, one firm's accountants will include the reps' salaries, the running costs of their cars and their expense accounts under 'sales costs', whereas the other may distribute these items under headings such as 'salaries', 'motor expenses' and 'travel and entertainment': neither one is necessarily better or more useful than the other, but if you attempt to compare the two without adjusting for the differences in the way the items are treated you will get a fairly meaningless result.

The balance sheet

This comes in two parts. What was traditionally the 'left-hand side', but is now more usually the top half, shows the net assets of the business: that is, the value on paper of everything it owns or is owed, less what it owes to others. The right-hand or bottom half shows how that value is apportioned among the owners, or in the case of long-term debts, those who have lent money to the business.

The arrangement is best understood if one looks at a sample:

Left-hand (top) half

	£	£
Fixed Assets		10,000
Current Assets	10,000	
Less Current Liabilities	5,000	
Net Current Assets	5,000	5,000
Balance Sheet value		15,000

Right-hand (bottom) half

	£
Owners' Capital (or share capital)	5,000
Profit and Loss Account	5,000
Reserves	5,000
Capital employed	15,000

Fixed assets

The top half of the balance sheet starts with the fixed assets of the business: everything it owns which is not part of its stock in trade and which is not a consumable: premises, machinery and office equipment, vehicles, tools etc. We shall be looking at how to assess the value of these to you, the purchaser, in Chapter 5, but their balance sheet or 'book' value is of interest for two reasons: it tells you what value the vendor attaches to them and enables you to calculate, when buying a company (and in the case of those items which can be depreciated) how much depreciation you have in hand to set against future profits. You should, however, be aware that companies may depreciate items on one scale in their accounts but on a different scale when computing their tax returns and you must, therefore, check whether the figures in the balance sheet are the same as those agreed with the taxman. The only point in having that depreciation in hand to offset against profits is that it will reduce your bill for corporation tax.

Property should be depreciated but frequently is not and may be in the balance sheet at cost, a valuable piece of information for you to check when negotiating the purchase. Some businesses have property revalued upwards from time to time, in which case the accounts will note the date of the valuation which is being used, but there is little pressure for small, private companies to revalue property as they are not open to a takeover bid. For public companies it is a different matter, as many learned to their cost in the boom years of the sixties; the City is full of bright young men with an eye open for a business whose shares are priced unrealistically low because it has not got round to revaluing its property at current prices.

The other fixed assets will have been depreciated according to one or other of the systems described (page 54). In the case of a sole trader or partnership you are, of course, interested in the balance sheet values only insofar as they affect your negotiations; it will be clear that a policy of depreciating fixed assets slowly will have enhanced past profits, whereas rapid depreciation will have lowered them. In the case of a company, where you are going to 'inherit' the book value which your predecessors attached to the assets, you will naturally want to know how much depreciation remains to be utilised or, if a piece of machinery, say, is overvalued because of rapid obsolescence, what paper loss you are going to make when you despatch it to the scrap merchant.

Current assets
This will be the next heading. Apart from any cash in the bank or in hand, current assets normally divide into stock and debtors. The stock figure will be that shown for closing stock in the trading account, which has already been discussed. In the case of sole traders and partnerships, the debtors do not directly concern you since it will be up to the outgoing owner to collect the debts. But in a company this is a very important figure. You will have to collect the debts that are outstanding at the time of the takeover and you will naturally want to be sure that you are not, in effect, buying any debt which you will not be able to collect promptly and in full. In theory, of course, any debts that are in serious doubt will have been provided for in the profit and loss account and deducted from the balance sheet debtors, but debtors who pay slowly could strain your resources in the future just as heavily as those who ultimately never pay, so it will be prudent to ask for an 'aged' list of major debtors. This will enable you to identify the larger items and to see how long they have been outstanding.

When assessing the records and potential of any business, even a sole trader or partnership, the debtors item provides useful information. Provided the business is not seasonal, in which case the total money owed will fluctuate according to the time of year, dividing the debtors into the sales will tell you how many months, on average, it is taking the business to collect its debts and, comparing year with year, whether the period of credit it gives is growing, shrinking or holding steady. This is crucial information for you in planning how you will run the business in future and assessing the resources you will have to invest in it, or the sums you will have to borrow.

The items under current assets are normally sub-totalled, and the following sub-total, for current liabilities, deducted in order to arrive at the net current assets which, added to the fixed assets figure, gives the value of the business.

Current liabilities

Current liabilities usually break down into creditors and bank or other short-term borrowings and, in the case of a company, the proportion of the profit which is due to be distributed as dividends and/or paid as corporation tax. Again, with a sole trader or partnership, these figures may be of academic interest, while with a company they are an integral part of the business which you are buying. But as the counter-balance to debtors, the creditors item gives an important guide to the amount of credit the business is getting from its suppliers. Assuming that there are no large bills included for fixed assets (a machine just installed and not yet paid for, or whatever) dividing creditors into the 'purchases' item under cost of sales in the trading account will reveal the length of credit which is being taken — you will have to establish whether suppliers will be as generous with you in the future or whether, by switching to others, you could contrive to pay more slowly.

As we saw when discussing interest charges in the profit and loss account, the extent to which the proprietor of a business has borrowed to finance it is a valuable indication of his bargaining position when it comes to selling; if the business is successful the owner is surely hoping that he will have a nice fat wodge of cash left after repaying all borrowings, and even if the business is unsuccessful he will certainly be aiming to clear the borrowings if at all possible. In the case of a company, the borrowings shown in the balance sheet are even more significant, for if you buy the company you will have either to continue to borrow that money, borrow it from another source, or replace it with funds out of your own pocket and/or those of other shareholders. If, as is most likely the case, the borrowing is in the form of a bank overdraft you must also bear in mind that in principle it can be recalled by the bank at any time; thus, you will have to assure yourself that the bank will be willing to continue the facility when you take over, or that you can replace it from other sources.

Balance sheet value

The total of fixed and current assets, less current liabilities, is the asset value or break-up value of the business — that is, in theory at least, the sum of money that would come to the proprietors if they closed it down and sold off all the constituent pieces on the date of the balance sheet. Three points must be borne in mind when looking at this figure. First, the value attached to the assets, especially the fixed assets, may well be highly artificial, and it certainly may not reflect their real worth or what the present owners expect to get for them. Second, as will be discussed in more detail in Chapter 6, the assets of a continuing business can only be valued in the context of the profit they generate. Finally, a balance sheet is a snapshot of the business's affairs taken at one particular moment; it is unsafe to assume that, for instance, the overdraft shown in the balance sheet is the maximum the business requires, or that debtors and creditors stay at the same levels year in and year out. It is also perfectly possible that the figures in the balance sheet are to some extent manipulated. For example, by early invoicing a business may increase the debtors figures or by holding back orders for materials or stock it may decrease the creditors. It is, therefore, important to compare the most recent accounts with those for earlier years to check, as far as possible, that the picture is not being artificially improved by a little surreptitious window dressing.

Ratios

We have seen how the balance sheet figures can be used to analyse the credit given or taken by a business. There are other clues to the business's health that can be derived from the balance sheet; they are especially valuable when you can compare them over several years and see which way the trend, if any, is going. Deducting current liabilities from current assets gives the working capital; dividing the total for current assets by the total for current liabilities gives the 'current ratio'. And to arrive at the 'liquidity ratio' you make what is sometimes called the 'acid test': you again divide current assets by current liabilities, but only after deducting the stock value from the current assets; for stock, after all, may be a long way from cash, and a business which has to sell all its raw materials and finished goods to pay creditors and lenders is not liquid in the sense that credit from suppliers, the continuation of its borrowing arrangements or a combination of both are essential to its continuance.

Capital employed

If the left-hand, or top, part of the balance sheet is a summary of the business's worth at a given point, the right-hand, or lower part, tells you how that worth is divided up among its owners. In the case of a sole trader the bottom half will normally be elementary, recording only the business's value as shown on the previous accounts with any profits which have increased it, or losses which have decreased it, during the current period. For example:

	£
Owners' Capital	5,000
Profit for year	1,500
	6,500

With a partnership the presentation will be more complicated: first, because the total has to be divided among the partners and, second, because the share of each partner is in turn divided into two categories: a current account and a capital account. The partners' *capital accounts* represent their original investment in the business and will normally stay the same from year to year, unless one or more of them injects further capital. Their *current accounts* are the accumulation of past profits less the portion of them which they have drawn. (Partners' salaries and any interest they are entitled to on loans to the business will normally be added to current accounts and for tax purposes they are lumped together with profits as income from the partnership.)

Even though the partners start by investing equal sums in the business, and retain an equal share of profits, the current accounts need not remain in step. Look at the capital and current accounts of Fred Frugal and Sid Swinger after their first year's trading. They each invested £10,000 at the outset and Fred also lent £2000 to the business.

Capital Accounts

	£		£
Frugal	10,000	Swinger	10,000

Current Accounts

Frugal		Swinger	
Brought forward	–	Brought forward	–
Share of profit	2,000	Share of profit	2,000
Interest on loan	250		
Salary	3,000	Salary	3,000
	5,250		5,000
Less drawings	1,500		4,995
	3,750		5

If you decided to buy the assets of Frugal and Swinger for, say, £30,000 the partnership would owe Sid £10,005, and Fred £13,750 plus the £2000 he had lent to the business, the surplus of £4245 would then be divided between the two partners equally.

A company's balance sheet also divides the worth of the business between the shareholders' original stake (the issued share capital) and profits that have been earned and retained in the business. But the categories and headings can vary a good deal. The first thing that concerns you, a prospective purchaser, is the structure of the share capital. In the case of most small businesses this is likely to be straightforward, perhaps 1000 ordinary shares of £1 each, but there are exceptions and you must know the rights attaching to each category of shares. The more usual ones are:

Ordinary shares. The ordinary shareholders are the owners of the business; ordinary shareholders will be entitled to one vote per share at the annual general meeting, to a share in the profit (if there is one) and if the company is wound up, any surplus is divided among them.

Non-voting shares. Normally the same as above, minus the right to vote. Usually a device for spreading the ownership of the company and the entitlement to a share of its profits more widely while retaining control in the hands of those who own ordinary, voting, shares. May sometimes be categorised as 'A' shares or given some other label to distinguish them from ordinary shares.

63

Preference shares. The point of a preference share is that its holder is entitled to first bite at the profits, but only up to a set point. Thus the owner of a 5 per cent preference share has to get his 5 per cent of the face or par value of the share before the ordinary shareholders are entitled to anything, but even if the company makes vast profits and the ordinary shareholders get a 20 per cent dividend, the preference shareholder only gets his 5 per cent. Moreover, since the preference shareholders' right to profit is limited, they would only get the face value of their share returned if the company was wound up — any surplus, or accumulated profit, goes to the ordinary shareholder.

Cumulative preference shares. The same as preference shares except that if the set dividend cannot be paid by the company in any year, the right to it is carried forward to future years.

Deferred shares. The holders do not receive any profits until the preference and ordinary shareholders have received some set level.

There may be other classes, founders' shares, A, B shares etc, differentiated by varying par values, voting powers etc. What they all have in common is that together they make up the capital of the company and are the equivalent of the partners' capital accounts.

Debentures and loan capital
Before moving on to the ways in which retained profits (the equivalent of current accounts in a partnership) can be described in the balance sheet, one further item must be mentioned. Debentures or other long-term debts may appear in the bottom part of the balance sheet although they are liabilities of the company rather than a part of its capital. The point is that such borrowings are for a set period and, therefore, while the company remains in existence it can count on keeping the funds until the redemption date. A debenture is a specific form of borrowing which entitles the lender to a set rate of interest, whatever the fortunes of the business, and gives repayment of his lending priority over the company's other creditors in the event of liquidation; but other, less rigorously defined, long-term lending may show up under 'loan capital' or some similar heading; the factor that puts it in the bottom part of the balance sheet rather than the top, under current liabilities, is that, unlike a bank overdraft, the company can be assured of

the use of the money for a set period and, usually, at a set rate of interest. It is therefore reasonable that it should appear in the lower part of the balance sheet, though it will always be accompanied by a note of the redemption date.

From the point of view of a prospective purchaser such long-term borrowing may be useful but, in calculating the value of the business, it must be borne in mind that when the time comes the money will have to be repaid out of profits or replaced from other sources and, in the meantime, payment of the interest is a fixed commitment. It should also not be forgotten that a debenture holder's priority over other creditors, especially shareholders, in the event of liquidation is usually absolute and you could well consider that this added to the risks of investing in the business.

Premium share issues
A company's share capital may have increased in the course of its existence by the issue of further shares to raise more capital or as a *scrip issue*. The point of a scrip issue is that by issuing existing shareholders with further shares, in proportion to the number they already hold, either free or at a discount to their market value, the company distributes profits it has accumulated without actually having to fork out cash; for a small company where the ownership is in a few hands it is a relatively pointless exercise since it does not alter the balance of ownership or voting power, but where the shares may be bought and sold it offers the shareholders a means of realising some of the accumulated profits to which they are entitled. If a company issues shares at a premium, ie, at a price higher than their face value, the surplus thus created in its balance sheet is normally labelled a share premium account.

Reserves
The capital of the company may also be increased by the creation of a *capital reserve*, that is, a reserve which cannot, by law, be distributed as profit to the shareholders (though it can be distributed in the form of an issue of shares as described above). The commonest reason for the existence of a capital reserve is the revaluation, at some time in the past, of a fixed asset at a profit. Thus, if Fred Bloggs Ltd (Builder) est 1895 woke up one morning to the realisation that their yard was now at the centre of a highly desirable residential area and worth rather more than the 100 guineas which it cost the original

Mr Bloggs in 1895, this paper profit would go into a capital reserve in the balance sheet. A share premium account is likewise a capital reserve.

The simplest way of dealing with the profits (or losses) which a company has accumulated over the years in balance sheet terms is to keep a running total of them in the profit and loss account. A firm which has always followed this policy has the most straightforward possible record of its career. Say that John Smith Ltd started business in 1978, made a loss that year of £2000, profits of £1500 in 1979, of £2000 in 1980 and a loss of £500 in 1981. Assuming that no part of the profits has been distributed as dividends and ignoring, for simplicity's sake, the fact that corporation tax would have been paid, the profit and loss account will stand at £1000 at the end of 1981.

For a variety of reasons, however, the sums available for the profit and loss account are often distributed among a variety of headings lumped together as *revenue reserves* (the point about a revenue reserve, including the profit and loss account, is that it is not part of the capital of the business and can be drawn upon to pay dividends in a bad year). Such revenue reserves may include a general reserve, which means what it suggests, or may be allocated to specific contingencies, towards the redemption of a loan or debenture, for example.

The essential thing to remember about reserves is that they do not consist of a nice little cache of money in the bank or under the chairman's mattress, they are a book-keeping convention. To see what the company has done with the capital and reserves listed in the bottom part of the balance sheet, you have to look at the top half which shows how the funds at the company's disposal have actually been deployed. All the bottom half tells you is what those assets are 'represented by' or 'financed by' on paper.

Return on capital
The two balancing figures at the foot of the top and bottom halves of the balance sheet are the capital employed by the company, and the final and most important figure that you can calculate from the balance sheet is the return that the company has been making from that capital. In the simplest terms, a business which employs a capital of £1000 to make a profit of £100 has a return on capital employed of 10 per cent. This calculation can be made regardless of the nature of the business. A sole trader's capital employed is the money he invested in the

business plus profits that have been left in it; a partnership's is the total of the partners' capital and current accounts; and a company's is, as we have seen, its capital plus its reserves and any long-term borrowing.

The rate of return on capital employed is a measure of the business's efficiency, and as well as seeing whether the rate of return is improving or worsening, you will want to check it against the figures for comparable businesses and, perhaps, estimate whether the same return could be obtained from less capital by, for example, moving to cheaper premises or whether the investment of more capital could produce a higher rate of return.

It must be remembered that the rate of return only has meaning if the assets, and therefore the capital employed, are valued realistically. If not, the rate of return in the past will be meaningless, and certainly not bear any resemblance to the rate of return you will get if you buy, for it is unlikely that you are going to buy the assets, or the business itself, at balance sheet value. Suppose the flourishing market garden owned by Harry Humus is valued in his balance sheet at £25,000 and makes a profit of £10,000. His return is a more than respectable 40 per cent. But, of course, Harry bought the land for a song during the agricultural slump of the thirties and it only stands in his books at £1500. Its real worth, together with the greenhouses he has built on it, his tools and the crops he has planted and cultivations he has carried out, is nearer the £100,000 he is asking for them. If you pay Harry's price, and run the business as efficiently as he has, you can expect a return on the capital you have employed of only 10 per cent — you might be better off putting your money in the post office.

When it comes to companies, the question is further complicated by the matter of 'gearing'. Take the case of Hill & Son Ltd. Its capital employed consists of 1000 ordinary shares of £1 each belonging to Jack Hill and his wife Jill, 10,000 5 per cent preference shares belonging to Jack Hill Senior and there is a 10 per cent debenture of £10,000 from one of the financial institutions plus retained profits and reserves of another £10,000: a total of £31,000. Its profits average £6000 a year, a return of about 19 per cent. But that return is not divided equally over the whole capital employed. Jack Senior gets £500 a year interest on his preference shares; the interest on the debenture is, of course, charged in the profit and loss account like interest on any other borrowing, so none of the profit goes to the debenture holders. The share of the capital employed which belongs to Jack Junior and Jill is the £1000-worth of ordinary shares plus all the retained profits and reserves. A quick calculation will show that Jack and Jill have a total of £11,000 invested in the company, and they are entitled to all of the £6000 profit except the £500 which goes to Jack's dad, so the return on capital is in fact 50 per cent. They might, with some force, argue that their ordinary shares were therefore worth, say, £50 each and if you paid this price for them *your* return would be around 9 per cent (the £50,000 you paid divided by the £5500 of profit your shares entitled you to).

Consolidated accounts

It was explained in the last chapter (pages 38-40) that a company with one or more subsidiaries will have to prepare consolidated accounts. In essence there is nothing complicated about these, they simply show the combined, net effect of the activities of the separate companies. Only the P&L and the balance sheet have to be consolidated, the trading accounts remain separate. The consolidated P&L takes the gross profits of the individual businesses and eliminates the effects of inter-company trading. If, for instance, the Crate Co sells 100 crates to its parent company, the Crock Co, at a profit of £50, and the Crock Co fills the crates with crocks and sells them at a profit of £500, then the trading accounts of the two businesses will show a total gross profit of £550, whereas the gross profit to the group is, in fact, £500 since when the Crock Co gave the Crate Co its £50 profit it was really only moving the money from one pocket to another.

The consolidated balance sheet may have to take care of two further aspects. Suppose that, though the Crate Co is a subsidiary of the Crock Co by virtue of the fact that the latter owns 60 per cent of its shares, nonetheless the other 40 per cent belongs to third parties; in order for the balance sheet to show the real value of the group the share of the profit belonging to these third parties has to be deducted each year. To deal with this, the entry showing the profit for the year in the balance sheet will be followed by a deduction of the amount 'attributable to minority interests', leaving a net figure which belongs to the parent company and is added to their profit and loss account or reserves.

The other eventuality that has to be covered is the possibility, even probability, that when the Crock Co bought its 60 per cent stake in the Crate Co it paid more than the face value of the shares. This surplus will appear in the consolidated balance sheet as 'Goodwill' or 'Goodwill on acquisition of Crate Co'.

SUBSIDIARY COMPANIES

If you are thinking of buying a business which is currently a subsidiary of a larger firm, you face the problem of disinterring an accurate picture of the subsidiary's affairs from its own accounts and the consolidated accounts of its parent. This can be a daunting task. This is not to suggest that large companies habitually fiddle the accounts of their subsidiaries, but to make the point that those accounts will have been affected by the fact that the business belongs to a larger entity. For example, it may well be that the parent has some overall policy on the depreciation of fixed assets, which may reflect their tax planning but not the realities of a particular subsidiary business. Many large groups charge their subsidiaries substantial fees for somewhat ill-defined things like 'management services' which, rather than representing a real service to the business (frequently they represent a genuine disservice), are a device for transferring profit from the periphery to the centre. If you are contemplating buying a business which has been paying such charges in the past you will have to try and decide how far they represent a real cost, which you would have to continue to bear, and how far they represent an effort by higher management to justify their existence and maintain themselves in the style to which they have become accustomed.

Things become even more complicated if the subsidiary has been involved in a lot of trading within the larger group. Though the parent's accounts will have been adjusted to eliminate the effects of this, the records of the subsidiary may well have been seriously distorted. Suppose, for example, that in the palmy days of the sixties Alpha Products set up a subsidiary, Beta Packaging, to manufacture packaging materials for its products. Now times are hard and Alpha has decided to dispose of Beta and buy its packaging on the open market. As a possible purchaser, you will want to discover first whether Beta has been so dependent on Alpha that it has never sought any other customers and has a product range entirely tailored to Alpha's requirements. It is clear that, as owners of Beta, Alpha could more or less determine its profit. They could decide to pay Beta the market rate for packaging and thus give it a chance to earn a reasonable profit, or they could force Beta to sell their goods to

Alpha cheaply and, in effect, transfer the potential profit to the parent company. In such a situation, it should be clear that the scope for manipulating the record is almost infinite.

Another area in which it may be difficult to judge the future performance of a business as an independent enterprise from its past performance as a subsidiary concerns its working capital. Most large holding companies, with access to loans at advantageous rates or, perhaps, their own cash resources, will prefer to act as 'banker' to their subsidiaries and minimise the overall borrowing by their entire group rather than seeing each subsidiary borrow separately to meet its own needs. Fair enough. But if you are contemplating buying a company that has had the benefits of this sort of arrangement or which, conversely, has been forced by a needy parent to part with every incoming penny as soon as it was received, then you will have to try and work backwards to see what its past performance would have been had it operated under more normal banking circumstances.

Balance sheet: Summary

The information that the balance sheet provides can be broken down into three basic items: it tells you how, historically, the present owners value the assets they are selling, how the money they have invested in the business has been tied up in those assets and how the money you pay for it will be distributed between them and their creditors. The first and third headings are, obviously, of use in negotiations; the second affects very directly the way in which you will run the business.

Take the first item to begin with. Suppose you are thinking of buying a business that has recently installed a lot of new plant or machinery; it is clearly handy, when negotiating with the vendors, to know what they paid for it, or if it has been in place for a year or two, how much of its value has already been written off against profits. You will be able to judge whether the value you attach to the equipment would involve them in biting the bullet and accepting a loss or whether, perhaps, you are being over-generous and in danger of paying a price which will represent a windfall to them.

The final item may equally well influence the way in which you tackle your negotiations. In the case of a partnership, for example, the balance sheet, if you see it, will show which partners have the most capital tied up in the business and may, therefore, be most anxious to sell; in the case of a company, where the accounts, by law, give details of the directors' shareholdings, such information could be equally useful. By looking at the debts of the business you will also be able to judge just how much the vendors will have to put in their pockets at the end of the day, again helpful knowledge to have at your fingertips when calculating the sort of offer that is likely to prove attractive to them.

The second item, the way in which the money currently tied up in the business has been invested — in fixed assets, in stock, in creditors etc — is the one which the various ratios aim at elucidating because this is vital knowledge for any business, whether it is being sold or not. From your point of view the important fact that can be deduced is the liquidity of the business and, thus, how much working capital you would need to keep it going. The liquidity of the business may also affect the vendor's attitude; if, for example, it requires more capital simply to continue its operations, he will clearly be more anxious to strike a bargain while the going is good, whereas if it will continue comfortably without requiring him to invest further resources, he may be inclined to sit back and wait for the best possible deal.

Let us take two examples, the Flush Co Ltd and the Fraught Co Ltd, both with the same balance sheet value, and see what can be deduced from their balance sheets, shown opposite.

Looking first at how the two businesses value their assets, it is clear that a startlingly large proportion of the Fraught Co's value is tied up in their £28,000-worth of machinery. If they have indeed just installed some wonderfully advantageous equipment that will revolutionise their performance, all may be well for them, but if they have simply been writing off the same kind of machinery as that possessed by the Flush Co more slowly than the latter then, clearly, they have been fooling themselves. That machinery may be the apple of their eye, but if we look at the second question, we can see that it is the root of a major problem.

For while the Flush Co has a current ratio of better than 2 : 1 (current assets of £26,000 against current liabilities of £12,000), the Fraught Co barely manages 1 : 1 and if we look at the acid ratio (by leaving stock out of the calculation) the Fraught Co has a ratio of virtually 1 : 2 whereas the Flush Co still manages a comfortable 1.75 : 1. In short, without an injection of working capital the Fraught Co is in bad trouble; in order to pay its

	Flush £	Fraught £	Flush £	Fraught £
Fixed Assets				
Property	20,000	20,000		
Machinery	15,000	28,000	35,000	48,000
Current Assets				
Stock	5,000	10,000		
Debtors	15,000	10,000		
Cash at Bank	6,000	—		
	26,000	20,000		
Less				
Current Liabilities				
Creditors	12,000	12,000		
Overdraft	—	7,000		
	12,000	19,000		
Net Current Assets	14,000	1,000	14,000	1,000
			49,000	49,000
Represented by				
Ordinary Shares			10,000	40,000
Profit & Loss Account			12,000	9,000
Loan			20,000	—
Reserves			7,000	—
			49,000	49,000

creditors it will have to borrow more from the bank or find additional cash elsewhere. If you buy the Fraught Co you will have to reckon on finding those other funds as well.

Things look slightly different, however, when it comes to the second half of the balance sheet. The owners of Fraught Co can at least comfort themselves that whatever you pay them for the business will go into their pockets; on the other hand, the owners of Flush Co have to pay off a loan of £20,000 (or accept that, if the loan stays in the business, the value will decrease in proportion to the long-term liability represented by the loan). There is, however, a further point to note. Even if a purchaser paid the balance sheet value for both businesses, the owners of the Flush Co would be making a profit of £19,000 on their original investment of £10,000 (the £12,000 they have set aside in the P&L plus the £7000 reserve) whereas the profit of the owners of the Fraught Co would be a mere £9000 on an investment of £40,000.

Given that the Fraught Co is clearly in trouble, its owners may be eager to cut what could very well become a loss; the owners of the Flush Co, on the other hand, can afford to sit back and wait for the right offer, confident that the business will not be a drain on their resources and that, all other things being equal, they can expect a handsome profit even after they have allowed for repayment of the loan.

Sources and application of funds

Most sets of accounts nowadays include a statement showing the source and application of funds. Such a statement reveals nothing which you cannot work out, given the accounts on which it is based, so even if it is not included you can calculate it for yourself. The point of such a statement is to analyse where a business's working capital (see page 62) is coming from and how it is being used. At its simplest, for instance, it might show that a business during the period in question had available to it £1000 in profits and that it had spent £500 of it on increasing its stock and £500 on new equipment.

In practice the calculations can appear paradoxical to non-accountants, and the vital key to understanding them is to grasp that they are an analysis of changes that have occurred between the beginning and the end of an accounting period. Thus an increase in stock, in creditors or in the amount of cash you have in the bank, though all are increases in assets, represent an application, or use, of funds; and an increase in debtors or overdraft, though increases in liabilities, represents sources of funds.

The sources of funds are:

New capital introduced, obviously, or new long-term loans.
The year's profit, equally obviously.
Depreciation. Although this was charged against profit in the P&L it did not actually absorb any cash and so has to be brought back into the calculation.
Money received from the sale of a fixed asset. The value of fixed assets is not involved in the trading account or P&L, but if you actually sell some of them the proceeds are, clearly, a source of funds.

Decreases over the period in stock, debtors, and other current assets.

Increases in creditors, overdraft or other current liabilities.

The applications of funds are:

Drawings made by the owner or profits distributed to shareholders.

Losses.

Taxation (in the case of companies).

Purchase of fixed assets.

Decreases in creditors, overdraft, long-term borrowing or other liabilities.

Increases in stock, debtors or other assets.

Looking at such a statement or, even more, a sequence of them, provides useful analysis of the way in which a business is heading, and, more especially, provides an early warning if it is sailing into danger. For instance, a firm working in an area of rapidly changing technology may be making good profits, but if it is spending them all on buying new equipment in order to keep pace with competitors, it may not have anything available for its owners by way of dividends. Or a business which, in a period of high inflation, is constantly increasing the value of its stocks, may be doing so by using the proceeds of depreciation; if this continues it will have no resources out of which to purchase new equipment when the old becomes worn out. A particularly common problem is 'overtrading'; this occurs when a successful business finds its sales running ahead of its ability to fund the cost of those sales and its overheads, and if it continues the business will simply run out of working capital.

Sources and application of funds: Summary

Like the profit and loss account, this is best looked at as a source of comparison and trends rather than of simple figures. The point of the exercise is to see the way in which the business is using, or being forced to use, its funds, and such movements are more easily and certainly detected over a period of time. For instance, it might not be a cause for concern if, in a single year, the funds derived from depreciation had been absorbed by an increase in debtors, but if such a movement is happening steadily over a number of years it is worrying, for it means that the cash reserve created by depreciation is disappearing into a sink of extended credit from which it may be difficult to retrieve it when new machinery is required. Clearly the main thing to discover and beware of is any tendency for funds generated by the business to be applied in ways which are likely to tie them up for long periods of time and thus diminish the business's liquidity and increase its need for working capital.

Chapter 5
Evaluating the Assets

Whatever the nature of the business you are buying and however you propose to go about buying it, the one concrete thing you will own when the purchase is complete are the business's assets. Its future profits, reputation, history and high standards are speculative or intangible: you cannot lay your hands on them, offer them to a bank as security or go out and sell them piecemeal. Since the assets are the one tangible, if necessary marketable, commodity you are getting in exchange for your money it is obviously important to evaluate them as carefully and realistically as possible. It may be that, if things go as you plan and hope, the profits will roll in over future years and the value of the assets will be of academic interest, but if things go badly then it is only by realising the assets that you stand any chance of recouping your investment. The purpose of this chapter is, therefore, to suggest how you should go about assessing, first of all, the tangible assets, fixed and current, and then those assets which are not in the balance sheet and have no value except as part of a going concern, but which nonetheless should be appraised with equal rigour.

Property

The first, and very likely the most valuable, asset to be considered is property, land and the buildings which stand on it. If the property is freehold then it may well represent not only the business's most valuable possession, but also the one which is most readily saleable, or which can most easily be used as security against which to raise money.

In considering any property, freehold or leasehold, you must examine it from two separate standpoints. First, what are its pros and cons as a home for the business you are thinking of buying? Is it the right size, conveniently laid out, in the right place (with good access to railway or trunk roads, etc)? The future of the business will obviously be affected if, for example, a factory is ill-suited for the processes it uses; or the warehouse on three floors so that endless time is wasted simply moving stock from one place to another; or if it takes your delivery van hours to struggle across the town centre to your major customers. In the same way, premises that are already over-crowded and have no room, or are unlikely to get planning permission for extensions, place a limit to the amount by which the business can grow, at least on its present site.

Setting aside the advantages of the property as a home for the business, you must also weigh up the chances of reselling the property or the lease, if you decide to move the business, if in the last resort the venture fails, or if you plan to consolidate it with another enterprise on a different site.

Freehold property
Estimating the market value of freehold property is a chancy and arcane skill, depending as much on the knack of judging the fluctuations of the property market as on any profound knowledge of architecture or structural engineering. Property men try and reduce this essentially intuitive process to a logical one by estimating or establishing the market rent for the property and then applying their current wisdom about the number of years' rent which it is economic to pay out for a purchase. The range in current use will, of course, depend upon interest rates and your view about their future movement — back into the arena of intuition and guesswork. One thing is certain: unless you are yourself an expert on property, you will do well to get expert advice, preferably from someone with local knowledge.

You or your solicitor will have to check out a business property in just the same way as you would a house you were buying to live in. You must make sure that it really does belong to the vendor and that it is free of mortgages or other charges; that there are no restrictive covenants in the deeds (rights of way through it, undertakings about the use or size of buildings erected on it etc); that the local authority has no long-term plans to build a bypass on it, and so on. In addition, especially in the case of a small business carried on from the present owner's home, you must make sure that planning permission has been given for the use to which it is being put, and that that use, or any possible extension of it, would not give rise to objections from the authorities or the neighbours which may limit its usefulness. You cannot afford simply to assume that all will be well. It is perfectly possible, for instance, that old

79

Peter Pointing never actually sought planning permission to use his back garden as a builder's yard or even to erect his joinery workshop in it later: no one objected because they all knew and liked Peter and, after all, one has to be neighbourly. But now that you are buying Peter's business, and proposing to install noisy new machinery, attitudes may be very different. People who tolerated Peter's business because they had assumed that it would end with his retirement may become intolerant if you propose to continue and expand it, and if no planning permission was given for business or industrial use in the past, it is likely to be very difficult indeed to obtain it now.

You will also need to have the buildings surveyed and probably valued by an independent valuer who is familiar with the area and current market prices. You should be sceptical about the value of buildings with very specialist designs or functions; to take an example, low damp windowless sheds may be ideal places to grow mushrooms, but if the mushroom business turns out to be less remunerative than you expect, you may have a job finding a buyer who has an alternative use for the sheds. Indeed, if they were originally wartime bunkers, say, with four foot concrete walls, their presence and the cost of demolition could actually diminish the value of the land on which they stand.

Leasehold property

If the business premises are leasehold rather than freehold the important consideration will naturally be the length and terms of the lease. First, however elementary it may seem, check that the vendor is entitled to transfer it (this will not apply where you are buying a company, since the benefit of the lease will go with the business); second, establish that you, in turn, will be able to transfer the lease to a third party. Not all leases are automatically transferable, and if you are not in a position to resell it then its value is enormously diminished. However reasonable the current rent may be, you must check the dates on which the lease comes up for renewal or the rent for review; a local valuer or estate agent will be able to tell you current rates for comparable commercial properties in the area which should give you at least some indication of the sort of rise the landlord is likely to ask for.

You should also check your liability, as tenant, for repairs and dilapidations, and it may be prudent to get the buildings surveyed to establish what work might be involved and its costs.

As with a freehold building, you must weigh up your chances of recouping, or even making a profit, if you decide to move the business or have to wind it up. Is it in a sought-after area, does its layout make it adaptable for different purposes, is the remaining lease long enough to make it an attractive proposition? Though it is difficult for a landlord to eject a sitting tenant, a lease is by its very nature a declining asset, unlike a freehold which is almost certainly an increasing one. The value of a lease therefore depends very much upon the importance to the business, or to yourself of having that particular site and no other. In the case of a High Street shop, the advantages may be clear, but elsewhere, a lease on a particular property may, in the last analysis, be a liability rather than an asset. Why should you pay for the privilege of taking over a lease on a property which, in comparison with other potential sites for the business, involves an un-economic rent, inconvenience or inefficiency? The only possible justification can be a certainty that you can resell the lease to someone else without loss.

Plant and equipment

In many instances it is not realistic to try and evaluate plant and equipment on the basis of their market value — they may not have one. The market for specialised tools or machinery, for example, is likely to be a narrow one and may be entirely dictated by chance considerations. It will vary enormously from trade to trade. The resale value of shopfittings, even of such things as freezers, is a fraction of their cost when new; a more specialised piece of equipment may not find a buyer at all other than the scrap merchant; in contrast, typewriters or motor vehicles have a relatively high and easily established second-hand value.

Much of the plant and equipment that you are buying may, therefore, have to be valued by you in the light of its worth to the business as a going concern. It has the advantage that it will almost certainly be cheaper than buying the same things new. On the other hand, if the machinery is old or obsolete, its very existence may be a disadvantage. At one end of the scale you might be picking up for a song desks, chairs and filing cabinets which, if you had to buy them new, would cost hundreds of pounds; at the other, you may be paying a high price for some large and antediluvian machine which, if the business is ever to flourish, will have to be dismantled and removed at considerable expense to make way for something more up to date.

Some checks you can make. Where items crop up regularly in the second-hand market you can establish their current price range. In the case of equipment that is relatively new, you can find out what it, or its equivalent, currently costs. Where complicated or older machinery is involved, you can ask to see the bills for servicing and repairs over the past year or two. You can also find out whether specialised bits of equipment have been, or are about to be, superseded by improved or cheaper versions or alternatives (not only will this render the old equipment uncompetitive, it is also likely to knock the bottom out of any second-hand value it has). But in many cases, you will, in the end, have to make some overall judgement — you cannot, realistically, try and value every stapler in the office or every spanner in the works.

When buying a company, there is one further consideration. All the plant and equipment will have been depreciated following one of the systems outlined on page 54, and it is important to establish what their book value is (and, if the system of depreciation followed in computing the company's past tax returns is different from that used in the published accounts, how much of their value remains to be written off for tax purposes). It could make quite a difference to your valuation of the assets if you know that, over the course of the next two or three years, several thousand pounds in depreciation could be set against taxable profits.

Stock

Stocks of materials are relatively easy to value; unless the business is in some especially esoteric line of trade, the materials it uses will probably consist of items which are relatively marketable and for which a current value is easily established. You must beware, of course, of paying too much for materials that are overstocked or outdated, damaged or perishable, or which are currently a drug on the market, but that apart, the vendor's request that you should purchase them at cost is likely to be reasonable. He may go further, and suggest that since the market price is now higher you should pay the replacement cost. In that case you will have to assess the strength of his bargaining position: if his stock is at a reasonable level, and if he could indeed dispose of it easily, then you will have to reach the best possible compromise; but if he is over-stocked, or if he is likely to have difficulty finding an alternative buyer, then you may decide to call his bluff. There is, for instance, unlikely to be any advantage in buying five years' stock of a particular item even at slightly below market price; the advantage of the low price will be overset by the cost of borrowing the money and storing the materials for a long period.

Work in progress and finished goods present a more complex problem. The essential thing to be sure of is that you will be able to sell the goods at a profit and within a reasonable period of time — what that period is will depend upon the commodity concerned. While six months' stock of cloth in a tailor's might be reasonable, six months' stock of orange juice in a grocery would be a nightmare. So in order to make a judgement, you may want to see not only an itemised stocklist, but also the past year's sales records. In some businesses, shops for example, where the business will not be carrying more than a few days' or weeks' stock, it is usual to agree that stock will be taken over at 'valuation', which in most cases means cost; in other instances, such as farms, where the stock to be taken over consists of crops planted and cultivations carried out, an independent valuer may be called in to fix a fair price.

Debtors

There are only two questions to ask about debtors: are they going to pay, and if so how long will it take them? Of course, the debtors that you are actually buying will not — unless the company is collecting its debts with unique lethargy — be the same as those who make up the debtors item in the last balance sheet. It usually takes a company weeks if not months from the end of an accounting period to the publication of an audited balance sheet, and it may be even longer from the end of a financial year to the date at which you take over, so the debts shown in the accounts will have been paid and replaced by a new lot. But provided the company is in a regular line of business with established customers, it is likely that the composition of the debtors will have remained much the same.

We saw in Chapter 4 how you could establish the average credit period which a business was extending. The important thing for you to establish is that the debtors at the date of takeover will not include any customers who are likely to prove exceptions to that average. An aged list of major debtors, which you can request and most companies should be able to supply, will identify, first, any individual or group of customers who accounts for a disproportionate amount of the company's sales and, second, any who are slow or reluctant payers. In extreme cases, where you have serious reservations about the likelihood of a substantial debtor paying up, you can ask for guarantees from the vendor against the eventuality of the debt turning bad.

Intangible assets

Many businesses have assets, often very valuable and real ones, which are by their nature intangible and are therefore not included in their balance sheets. Most book publishers, for example, do not attach any book value to the copyrights they lease or own, even though the possession of those copyrights is fundamental to their business. Similarly, patents or licences to exploit a particular product or process are unlikely to be valued in the balance sheet, and the same applies to contracts.

Even though such items have no book value, the vendor is likely to argue with vehemence, and on the face of it some justice, that you should pay for them handsomely. The suggestion must be treated with the greatest possible caution, for such assets are different in kind from things like property, debtors etc in that they may have a value only while the business continues in being, but may be virtually worthless if you have to put them on the market. Copyrights or patents may revert to the licensors in the event of the licensee's business collapsing and may, in any case, be of value only to a small number of other people. In short, intangible assets are likely, if it comes to the crunch, to prove unrealisable as well.

Goodwill

You will, of course, have to pay something for such intangible assets, even if they amount to no more than the business's contacts with customers or suppliers or its reputation in the trade; for unless you are buying a moribund or failed business, you will certainly pay a price which exceeds the book value of its assets. The surplus is given the much misunderstood label of 'goodwill'. Goodwill is in essence nothing more than an accountant's term for an item in the accounts that cannot find a place under any other heading.

Let us say that last year you purchased a flourishing restaurant business for £20,000. The lease of the premises was valued at £10,000 and the kitchen equipment, cutlery and crockery, table linen etc amounted to another £5000. Since the business was making a profit of £11,000 a year you reckon you got a bargain; but when your accountant comes to make up your accounts for the year he is faced with a difference of £5000 between the value of the assets you purchased and the price you paid and in order to get the balance sheet to 'balance' he will add £5000-worth of goodwill to the top part of the balance sheet. If you leave it in the accounts, at cost, it will, in the case of a company or partnership, be part of the capital of the business and cannot be distributed as profit. Of course, if you come to sell the business again, or go to your bank manager for a loan, that goodwill figure will be immediately discounted by anyone who has to appraise your accounts. If the business has been going badly, then the figure simply reveals that you paid too much for it; if it has been going well then the fact will be revealed by its profits. For this reason, if no other, most businesses like to get any goodwill element out of their accounts as quickly as possible by writing it off against profits. Many people, however, take goodwill literally and interpret it as the reputation, patronage and success enjoyed by a business. But if you are asked to pay for the goodwill of a business do translate the suggestion into its real meaning — goodwill is no more than an assessment of the likelihood that the business will make a profit for you in the future, a very important calculation, as we shall see in the next chapter, but one quite different in its nature from the judgement of the market value of a business's tangible assets. This does not mean, naturally, that you ignore the 'assets' that are likely to determine the future profitability of the business, just that you must clearly distinguish them from those assets which are tangible and, if necessary, saleable. On that basis it is worth trying to assess those assets under various headings.

Customers and suppliers
A business's reputation boils down, in the end, to no more than the extent to which its customers are likely to continue to patronise it and the degree to which its suppliers trust it and are, therefore, willing to give it the best terms and service.

With a small business, the important thing to try and judge is how far the business's present reputation and success depend upon its owner rather than being intrinsic to the business itself. Is the little grocery shop profitable because most of its customers have known the present owner, and his father before him, and will they, if you take over, desert to the nearest supermarket in droves? Does that modest engineering works continue to get subcontract work from the big firm up the road because it suits them or simply because the respective managing directors went to school together?

One point to look out for is how far a business is dependent on one or two large customers or suppliers. It may be very nice that a small print shop can get all the work it can cope with from the large advertising agency nearby; but what happens if the agency falls on hard times, or appoints a new print buyer who has his own favourite suppliers? The little print business may have become so insulated from the market place that it has neither the staff nor the contacts to go out quickly and find new business. It may in the short term lead a harder and more fraught life if it relies upon a variety of smaller customers and has to keep a sales staff to hunt up new ones, but in the long run it may be a safer and better life.

The same applies to suppliers. A business that has got into the habit of relying on one or two suppliers and perhaps turned away representatives of their rivals so regularly that they have simply given up bothering to call, can easily find itself in difficulties if its sole supplier goes out of business, decides to stiffen its terms or reorganises its operations. If, therefore, you are contemplating buying a business which seems to have too many of its eggs in one or two baskets, you should at the very least check up on the baskets. Go and talk to major customers and suppliers and sound out their attitude to the business, should you decide to take over. And, rather than congratulating yourself on finding a business which is so well situated, have a look around the market place and try and judge how easy it would be for you to replace that big customer or find an alternative supplier.

Style and personality

It is a fact of life that even very large businesses can depend for their success or failure on the personality of one man or woman, and this holds equally true for small businesses. This is not a factor to be ignored, for the personality most likely to be involved is that of the present owner, by definition the one part of the business you will not be able to take over.

At the most basic level, a shop may do well simply because the owner always has a cheerful word for the customers. You may be a much better businessman than he has ever been, but are you capable of finding a new piece of gossip every week for this customer and a fresh risqué joke for that one? It is best to be as realistic about this side of things as possible: many businesses are, by their very nature, dependent as much on personality as on business skills, and if you have the wrong kind of personality for the job you will not only fail at it, you will be miserable too.

Staff
An efficient and happy staff is, it should go without saying, one of the most important assets any business can possess. The fact that most of what follows deals with potential problems and difficulties should not be taken to infer that these should be your main consideration, only that there is little to be written for the purchaser who takes over a business which involves no personnel problems — except to congratulate him on his good fortune.

Your inspection of the accounts (see Chapter 4) will have provided the basic information you need about the current wage and salary bill and the rate at which it has been increasing. In a business which is large enough to employ any kind of middle management, you will want to meet those involved and make your own assessment of their strengths, weaknesses and suitability for the job. If your interest in acquiring a business progresses beyond casual interest to serious negotiation, it is very much to your advantage to do everything you can to minimise the uncertainty, rumour and fear inevitably current in any business which is about to change hands. The last thing you want to take over is a business which has been disrupted and, perhaps, has even lost key employees as a result of an impending change of ownership. Try, therefore, to avoid spreading alarm or fuelling rumours when you meet employees; but on the other hand, avoid making any commitments you may not wish, or be in a position, to keep.

CONTRACTS OF EMPLOYMENT AND REDUNDANCY
If your plans for the business involve changes or cutbacks in staffing, then you will certainly want to establish where you

stand vis-à-vis the employment laws, and in particular what the position will be over any redundancies among the labour force.

Every employee has, or should have, a contract of employment with his employer. This will, among other things, state the period of notice that has to be given by either side; on the employer's part it is normally one week for each year of service. In addition, every full-time employee gains an entitlement to statutory redundancy pay after two years' service. If a business is sold as a going concern, and this can be held to apply even if on paper it is only the assets which change hands, then the employees' contracts of employment normally remain valid and, for the purposes of redundancy etc, their period of service with the old employer is added to that with the new employer to form one continuous period of employment.

So where do you stand as the potential purchaser of a business? If the present employer is a sole trader then the contract of employment is a personal one between him and the employees and will usually be terminated if he closes the business or dies. If, however, you buy the assets of the business while he is still alive and continue running it in the same place, you may be held to have taken over the contract of employment and the liability for redundancy pay with it. Naturally, if you want to continue employing the same staff on the same work all is well and good. But if you are planning staff cuts, or even, for instance, envisage moving the business to a different location or changing its nature, then you should make certain that the question of notice to the employees and any entitlement to redundancy pay is the responsibility of the outgoing owner.

The same sort of considerations apply in the case of a partnership, except that the death of a single partner does not usually cancel the contract of employment or invalidate the redundancy entitlements of the employees.

Again, when a company sells off a particular operation, or even all of its assets, responsibility for its obligations to its employees normally remains with it, even, technically at least, if it goes into liquidation. If, however, a newcomer takes over a factory, say, and continues to use it for the same purpose and employs the same staff, then it may be argued that the incoming owner has taken over the obligations of the outgoing one as far as the work force is concerned, even if the transaction between the two amounted to no more than the sale of property and equipment. Of course, if ownership of a company itself changes hands then the new owners take on all contractual and statutory obligations to employees along with all the company's other assets and liabilities.

If redundancy is going to become an issue, then it is one that must be taken into account in the negotiations with the vendor right from the start. Employment law is complex, and you will do well to seek professional advice; the essential thing is not to leave it until after you have taken over to sort it out, for it may be that, in law, the vendor is responsible and even if the position is confused you are likely to lose whatever bargaining strengths you had vis-à-vis the vendor if you leave the issue aside until the sale is completed.

A special case arises over any employee who has a service contract. This is a matter likely to arise only in the case of fairly senior staff, either where they have an existing contract or, sometimes, when the vendor proposes that the signing of a service contract should be a part of a takeover in order to ensure the security of his colleagues after his departure. In theory, a service contract is a double-edged weapon, by which the employee guarantees his services for a given period in return for a guarantee of employment for the same period, normally at an agreed salary. In practice, however, few businesses would be attracted by the idea of enforcing their side of the bargain against a senior member of staff who wished to leave whereas, if the situation is reversed, the employee can hold the business to the terms of the contract by insisting on severance pay. From a purchaser's point of view, therefore, employees with service contracts are a mixed blessing: the agreements certainly constitute some sort of commitment by the individuals concerned towards the business, but, in contrast to the employer's commitment, which is binding and enforceable, the employees' amounts to little more than a moral obligation.

PENSIONS

One final point to check, as far as staff are concerned, is the pension arrangements.* If the business is in the state pension plan then you know where you are as far as the current rate for employers' contributions go. But if the business has, in the past, opted out, as many employers have in order to set up a private pension scheme, then this will need looking at in considerable detail. Such schemes have by law to provide certain minimum benefits which at least match those offered by the state scheme,

---

* At the time of going to press (December 1985) it was unclear how this issue would be affected by the government's proposed changes in the social security system.

and though they will probably be financed by a combination of employer's and employees' contributions, the burden of making up any shortfall will almost certainly be borne by the employer. Despite the advice of actuaries and others, and the trusteeship of institutions, such private pension schemes frequently suffer from underfunding — in a small company it only needs one employee in the mid-thirties to leave and be replaced by one in the mid-fifties for the finances of the whole operation to go awry, for example.

If you are considering buying a business which has embarked upon a private pension scheme you will be well advised to get the most up-to-date report available on its position or even commission a separate report. Making good a shortfall in funding can involve the business in finding, at relatively short notice, large sums in cash and, if ignored, it is a problem that can only get worse.

Conclusion

This chapter has dealt with the assets of a business under two main headings: those which are in the balance sheet and which are, if it comes to the point, saleable by some means or another; and those which, while they may be even more important and potentially more valuable to the business, only have worth in the context of a continuing business, in other words as the resources from which future profits will be earned. These two headings form the basis of the next chapter, for the two principal yardsticks by which a buyer can judge the worth of a business are its 'break-up', or asset, value and its future profitability.

Chapter 6
What is the Right Price?
Can you Afford it?

If you have followed the advice in the last two chapters you will
have examined the track record of your prospective purchase,
weighed up how far you can improve upon it in the future, and
taken a long, cold look at the assets of the business. You now
have before you the basis for two quite distinct — and often
very different — valuations. It is a bit like buying a race horse.
You have a mass of information in the accounts, the business
equivalent of the form book, which tells you what ought to
happen in the future and how much prize money, in the form
of profits, you can hope to collect; but it is always possible that
a business, like a horse, will not fulfil its promise — the going
may prove too heavy, you may turn out to be a poor trainer or
jockey, it may be pipped at the post by a rival. In that case you
have to calculate what your purchase is going to be worth to a
tough minded horse coper or, if the worst comes to the worst,
in the knacker's yard of bankruptcy.

Asset values *v* potential profit

Which of these two values — assets or potential profit — is the
real one?

As with most important questions, the answer is that 'it all
depends . . .'. Take first a highly successful business with
scarcely an asset worth the name in hard, balance sheet terms;
something like Donald Deal's estate agency, let us say, with a
virtual monopoly of the business in a desirable residential area,
an excellent reputation and, consequently, an enviable record of
profit going back several years. The asset value of the business,
which boils down to a bit of office equipment and a supply of
'FOR SALE' boards is negligible and Donald would laugh in
your face if you offered him ten times the sum. Clearly, in a
case like that what you are evaluating is the business's position
in the market place as reflected in its past performance and the
chances that you will be able to continue the run of success.

At the other extreme is something like agriculture where

prices are determined by the value of the — literally — underlying assets in the form of land. The value, acre for acre, of Farmer Slouch's farm which loses thousands of pounds a year is very little different from that of the prosperous Farmer Swift next door.

The rule of thumb for evaluating a business like Donald Deal's is based on a multiple of his annual profits — the actual figure used (the number of years' profits that make up the purchase price) will of course vary, depending on the general economic climate, the current rate of inflation and interest, and the degree of risk involved.

If that sounds forbiddingly technical, do not be put off. The easiest way of looking at it is to suppose, as well may be the case, that you will have to borrow most or all of the money needed to purchase the business. In most cases that means that you are going to pay interest at around 2 or 3 per cent above the current minimum lending, or base, rate. For the sake of simplicity, let us say that base rate is 12½ per cent and you can borrow at 2½ per cent over, or 15 per cent. Clearly, in these circumstances, it will not be a sound proposition to pay six times earnings for a business, since for every £600 you invest you will be getting back only £100 in profits and of that, £90 is going in interest payments. If, on the other hand, you pay three times earnings then you have only to invest £300 to get your £100 profit, and of that £100 only £45 is going in interest. The calculation is naturally based as much on expectations of future interest rates as on current rates, and is thus a reflection of the economic climate in general.

A high rate of inflation has much the same effect as high interest rates — after all, if money is losing its value at the rate of 15 or 20 per cent a year, then a return on investment of less than that figure represents a loss in real terms. As we will see later in the chapter, an inadequate profit will quickly be absorbed simply by keeping the business going in a period of inflation. It is, however, also true that a long period of inflation has a beneficial effect if you are borrowing in order to buy a business. Suppose that you have borrowed £10,000 and invested it in a sound and steady business where both profits and asset values stay in step with inflation. Suppose, furthermore, that over a ten-year period inflation averages 10 per cent per annum and interest rates stay steady at 15 per cent. If you have paid, let us say, a price equal to four times annual profits in the year of purchase then in year one your profit will be £2500 and your interest bill will be £1500 or 60 per cent of profits. In year ten, however, your profit will have more than doubled to over £5000 whereas your interest bill will have stayed the same at £1500, or less than 30 per cent of profit. The snag in this argument is that while profits may keep pace with inflation, maintaining their 'real' value, it is in the nature of most assets to decline in 'real' value while the cost of replacing them increases.

One asset, land, does not decline in value but, experience suggests, it can be relied upon to appreciate and keep pace with the diminishing value of money. That is why the value of Farmer Slouch's property is comparatively uninfluenced by his lamentable failure to make a profit out of it. Slouch's farm is, thus, a less risky investment than Donald Deal's estate agency in the sense that the land will always be there and will retain its 'real' value however incompetent you turn out to be as a son of the soil. The degree of risk involved will have some influence on the relationship between profits and price, but it is not an overwhelming one; if you continue to run up losses at the same rate as Farmer Slouch, it will not take many years for the accumulated losses to overtake the value of the assets.

Between the extremes represented by these two examples lie most of the businesses you are likely to encounter: businesses which confront you with the problem of reconciling two values, based on entirely different calculations and each in its own way entirely 'correct'. You must remember, too, that the vendor will also be looking at two sets of figures but, perhaps, from a rather different angle.

Let us take an example in the shape of Mr Rose, the nurseryman, whose business you are eager to buy. Both parties start from the same point, Mr Rose's accounts for the past few years. These show profits running at £15,000 a year and assets valued at £40,000, ignoring, for the sake of simplicity, both debtors and creditors. In the last balance sheet the assets break down as follows:

	£
Fixed Assets	
Property (at cost)	20,000
Buildings, Plant and Machinery	
(after depreciation)	15,000
Current Assets	
Stock (at cost)	5,000

Mr Rose will certainly look at these items through rose-tinted glasses and he will see something like this: the property, well, it was bought 20 years ago when it was right on the fringes of town, now it's in the middle of a nice residential district and you would almost certainly get planning permission to develop it for housing; you could get four bungalows on the land and the going rate for building plots is £7500 apiece. The house which goes with the business has also increased in value as the neighbourhood has developed; it must be worth, say, £30,000. Ergo, the property is worth £60,000. As for the buildings and machinery, it would cost at least £20,000 to build greenhouses like that at today's prices and though some of the equipment is a bit long in the tooth, it's certainly worth a lot more than its balance sheet value; the buyer should think himself lucky if he gets the lot for £25,000. As for the stock etc, an awful lot of work has gone into caring for the young plants and shrubs and a lot of the garden furniture was bought several years ago at prices way below the current figures; given that the stock is worth maybe £12,000 at retail prices he'd be a fool to let it go for less than £7000. Adding the whole lot up, Mr Rose reckons that it would be a steal if anyone paid less than £92,000 for the business.

You, on the other hand, have read Chapter 5 of this book, and see things rather differently. It is always possible that Mr Rose is right about the value of the land for housing, but he has not actually applied for planning permission so it is only a guess that it would be granted. In any case, you want to be a nurseryman not a property developer and it is obvious that a large part of the business's success is due to its situation: if you moved it to a less central site you would probably lose a lot of the trade. The land is worth perhaps £10,000 and the house, unmodernised and dilapidated, £20,000. As for the buildings, the heating system is a monument to waste; it would be cheaper to stoke it with pound notes than the oil which it consumes by the barrel. The first thing that would have to be done — at considerable cost — is to replace it with something a bit more up to date. The same goes for the machinery; well maintained it may be but much of it would not have been out of place in Mr McGregor's garden. The stock of plants has obviously been tended with care but, having been to horticultural college, you are aiming a bit higher than the wallflowers and wisteria which seem to have been Mr Rose's stock in trade. If there is going to be room for the exotica you plan to plant, you will have to get rid of the lot at a knock-down price, and the reason that the garden furniture has been sitting around for years is that no one wants stuff like that any longer. All in all, a fair value would be £45,000 for the lot.

Mr Rose applies the same sort of optimistic thinking to his profit. £15,000 a year would not be a great return on assets for which you have paid over £90,000, he has to admit. But think of the hidden profits. You can live rent free in the house that goes with the business, and he has always grown all his own vegetables and charged things like domestic lighting, heating and rates to the business, and of course had all his private motoring for free. When he takes all that into account, he explains, the real profits are at least £20,000.

You, with Chapter 4 fresh in your mind, take a rather different view. When you inquired about the remarkably low wage bills in Mr Rose's accounts, it emerged that Mrs Rose tended the cash register and did all the book-keeping and that most of the manual labour around the place had been done by assorted young Roses in return for a bit of pocket money. You, as a bachelor, have neither wife nor children and do not much fancy living in a house that, from the evidence, has not been redecorated since 1939 and lacks all the mod cons you take for granted. Moreover, you are not going to pull many birds in the 15-year old Land Rover which serves the Rose family for transport. Even if, with your new ideas and modern methods, you improve the efficiency of the business and its profitability quite spectacularly, you have got to reckon on hiring at least one full-time and one part-time employee, you will have to spend quite a bit on the house and will also want a vehicle that is more in keeping with your life-style. Given costs like these, you reckon you will be lucky if, for the first few years at least, you end up with a profit of more than £12,500 in your accounts. Add on another £2500 for benefits in kind (less, admittedly, than Mr Rose calculated he was getting, but then you are only housing, feeding and transporting yourself, not a family) and you are looking at total earnings of perhaps £15,000.

To summarise, Mr Rose's view of his business goes something like this: he has assets worth £92,000 on which he has been making a real profit of £20,000 per annum, an asking price of £100,000, or five times earnings, does not seem out of the question. Maybe he will have to be prepared to bargain a bit and come down to £90,000, but that, surely, must be rock bottom.

Your conclusions are rather less optimistic. You have calculated that the assets are worth £45,000 at the outside and you will be lucky to make more than £15,000 a year out of them. Moreover, you are going to have to spend at least £15,000 on new equipment, modernising the house, and for working capital etc so, if you paid out the full value of the assets you would be investing a total of £60,000, or nearly four times the potential profits. At that sort of figure you are dangerously near the point at which, if you have to borrow the cash, interest payments would eat up most of your profit.

The situation is a deadlock. In Mr Rose's eyes the asset value gives the business a worth which is quite out of proportion to its profitability; from where you stand its poor profitability reduces its value below even your valuation of its assets, a figure which is only half Mr Rose's estimate.

How can such an unbridgeable gap occur? To start with, Mr Rose has made the common error of trying to have his cake and eat it too. Suppose he is right about the potential development value of the land — in that case, his greeenhouses are, in effect, so much junk to be removed, his tools are worth whatever a scrap dealer will pay for them and his stock of plants only has a value if it can be sold off before the bulldozers move in. In short, you cannot grow begonias and bungalows on the same patch of soil. Mr Rose must decide whether he is selling a nursery business or a housing site. It is hard for Mr Rose, who has long since repaid the modest loan he raised to buy the business and is making a comfortable living out of it, to see that his asking price is totally out of line with the profits that a purchaser could expect to make, and that if and when those profits improve it will be in large part due to investment in modernisation and improvement.

The most serious mistake that you, as a purchaser, can make is to be persuaded that Mr Rose's viewpoint is the right one. Mr Rose is asking you to assess the business's value to a speculative builder or another nurseryman with a brood of hard-working kids, whereas what you are, or should be, concerned with is what is is worth to you.

The answer is that to obtain the £15,000 profit, you are willing to invest £50,000, roughly three and a half times earnings. Of that £50,000 you have estimated that £15,000 would go on modernisation, improvements and working capital, so you have £35,000 which you can afford to offer Mr Rose. That is not only below Mr Rose's very optimistic valuation of the assets, but also below your more realistic one. Nonetheless it is the correct answer. To see why that should be so, let us look at what would happen if you were to weaken and fork out the £45,000 which was the asset value that you calculated. Under those circumstances you face a dilemma: either you do the modernisation programme you planned, in which case your total investment goes up to £60,000, or you stick within your £50,000 limit and hope for the best.

Now if you opt for the first alternative, you face interest charges (at an annual rate of 15 per cent, let's say) of £9000. That leaves £6000 of the profit for you to live on, and remember that £2500 of that was in the form of benefits in kind — you only have £3500 in your pocket to spend.

If you choose the second option you are in even worse trouble. True, your investment is only £50,000 so the interest charge is reduced to £7500 but there is no way that you can match the £20,000 profit that Mr Rose was getting out of the same, unmodernised assets. Your benefits in kind only come to £2500, not the £5000 he got out of the business, and you have to pay out at least £5000 in wages, leaving you after interest with a meagre £2500 cash at the end of the day.

We have gone into the case of Mr Rose's nursery in some depth in order to make the point that, where there is a gulf, or even a gap, between the asset value of a business and the value based on its profitability, it is the latter which a purchaser must treat as the real value. In the context of a continuing business an asset has a value only insofar as it is a source of profit; the fact that it exists and has a market value may underwrite the risk of a business investment but the benefits that the security gives will only become real if the asset is sold.

Gearing

In an orderly world the sort of price : profit formula described would be revised once a month and published in the *Financial Times*, making it simple to calculate the market price for any business. Sadly, things are not so simple. Apart from the sort of considerations we have already discussed, there are other factors which not only separate one kind of business from another, but also one buyer from another buyer.

The first of these is the fact that you may actually have the money needed to buy the business rather than having to borrow it. This may not make very much difference in theory, but in practice the relationship between the owner's funds invested in a business and the borrowed money, the gearing as it is called, is fundamental.

Let us suppose that you have agreed to pay £30,000 for a business earning profits of £10,000 and that you expect the profits to continue at the same level. Now if you actually have, say, £25,000 in your bank account and only have to borrow the balance of £5000, your gearing ratio is low. The return on investment, at 33 per cent, is high, and a very high proportion of the profits will stay with you, in the form of income or increased assets even after you have paid interest on the £5000 you have borrowed. If, for example, the interest rate is 15 per cent you will only have to part with £750 a year out of the £10,000 profit and you will probably be able to reduce that fairly rapidly by repaying the loan out of the balance of the profits.

Let us now imagine that the business is almost three times as large, costing £75,000 and producing profits of £25,000, but that your own funds still total only £25,000, necessitating borrowings of £50,000. If things go on as before then your interest bill is going to be £7500, leaving you with a return of £17,500 on your investment of £25,000. Clearly, in such circumstances the high gearing has worked to your advantage. You have in effect used someone else's money to increase the earning power of your own funds.

But look, for a moment, at what happens when things do not go according to plan and let us suppose that the business's value decreases by one third. If you decide, or are forced by falling profits, to sell the first, smaller business for the lower price of £20,000 then you are left, after repaying the £5000 loan, with £15,000 or 60 per cent of your original capital. But in the case of the larger, highly geared business, the sale price of £50,000 is just sufficient to repay your borrowings and you have lost your own £25,000 in its entirety.

High gearing, in short, is an advantage when things go well, but it increases the risks dramatically when things go badly. In weighing up the value of a business to you, therefore, you must consider the degree of gearing that will be required and, in particular, the risk it may involve.

What is a profit?

It is a common assumption that the annual profits of a business consist of a cache of banknotes under the chairman's mattress which he can and will fork out if his arm is twisted hard enough.

Since the profits of your business are what you are going to have to live on, it is as well to be clear at the outset exactly what form they are likely to take and how much of them is going to be available in ready cash to pay the butcher and to buy the kids' clothes.

It is fairly obvious that if a business is expanding it will, unless it is raising or borrowing money from outside, be ploughing back a proportion of its profit. What is perhaps less obvious is that inflation forces exactly the same process on a business whether it likes it or not, especially if it is one which involves carrying substantial stock of goods or materials. If you buy a business with £10,000-worth of stock and, after a year, have exactly the same number of items in your stock room, which, after inflation, have cost you £10,500, that extra £500 will, all other things being equal, have to be found out of your profit. The same sort of thing happens with fixed assets like machinery: suppose that your business owns a new machine for which you have paid the exact book value of £5000. If you write that machine off over five years in a straight line (see Chapter 4) then you will have deducted the depreciation of the machine from your profits and have £5000 tucked away to buy a new machine — all well and good, except that new machines now cost not £5000 but, after five years of inflation at an average rate of 7 per cent, over £7000. Again the additional £2000 will have to come out of profits and, this time, out of taxed profits.

It is true that the increased value of the stock and of the more expensive new machine when you buy it will be reflected in the value of your assets as shown in the top half of your balance sheet, and the proportion of the profit which you have set aside to buy them will be added to the profit and loss account in the bottom half. What you are in fact doing is taking a proportion of your profit and setting it aside to ensure that the value of your assets increases in pace with the rate of inflation. In other words, you have to be sure that the business with £10,000-worth of stock and the £5000 machine can spare £900 out of its first year's profits (£500 for the additional cost of the stock plus £400 towards the higher cost of a new machine) if you are simply to stay in the same place. If the profits of the business also keep pace with inflation at 7 per cent they clearly have to start at more than £13,000 if you, too, are to maintain your standard of living, for otherwise a disproportionate share of the increased profits will have to go back into the business rather than being available for you to draw, and that share will increase every year until it is absorbing all the profit.

The importance of this sort of consideration will vary enormously with the nature of the business; for something like a market stall, for instance, the value of the stock and the fixed assets is so low in relation to the turnover and profits of the business it is scarcely a consideration; in manufacturing business, on the other hand, it may be a vital one. If you look at the statement from past accounts showing the sources and applications of funds, you will be able to see how important it is in the business you are considering and, indeed, whether the previous owners have paid sufficient attention to it.

Working capital

If the business you have bought was that of a sole trader or partnership then you have (remember Chapter 3) bought only the fixed assets and the stock of the business. Before you see any money coming into your bank account there may well be bills and wages to be paid, further stocks to be purchased etc. Even if you have bought the share capital rather than just the assets of a company and thus have the benefit of cash coming in from debtors, it does not follow that this will in the short term balance the sums due to creditors and other expenses. If you have calculated the company's liquidity ratio from its past accounts (see Chapter 4) you will have some idea of your needs in this area, but whatever the nature of the business you are buying you will certainly need to do a cash flow forecast for the next year, or more, in order to establish what the peak requirement for cash is going to be, and when it will occur.

To see why this is necessary, and how it is done, we will suppose that you are on the brink of buying a nice, well-situated toyshop in your native town. It is now mid-March and the proposed date for completing the sale is 5 April. You have all but agreed a price, let's say £20,000, to include the stock in the shop at the date of completion which will, valued at cost, amount to £5000, give or take a hundred pounds or so either way. All well and good you may think: as I sell the stock I will have cash available to replace it. But wait a moment: a toyshop doesn't have a steady, regular flow of business month in and month out; the Christmas trade is going to be crucial to you, and big sales in November and December mean big stock purchases in September and October. A bit of research with the outgoing owner shows that, on the basis of past experience, you can expect sales in November and December to run at £7000 a month, double the normal rate of £3500 a month, and that your bills from suppliers in September and October will therefore be £4000 each month rather than the usual £2000. You also have to reckon, realistically, that at the outset you will have to order at least £1000-worth of stock to make sure that you always have a full range available. You also have to allow for the fact that your first quarter's rent, say £750, is due the day you move in and the next year's rates will become payable at the beginning of May. Allowing for monthly drawings of £600 and an average overhead bill of £250 a month, your cash flow would be as shown overleaf.

If those figures are right it certainly looks as if you are buying a useful little business, but they also show that in a couple of weeks' time you are going to need, not just the £20,000 to complete the purchase, but another £1100 of working capital. Moreover, you are not going to get much of that money back until November and, indeed, come October, you will need even more.

If you add into this calculation things like new equipment, perhaps redundancy payments or, in the case of a company, corporation tax on last year's profits, it is surprising how high the peak can go above the simple purchase price. In many cases the calculation will be longer and much more elaborate, but it is nonetheless vital, and unless you have planned for, and taken steps to secure, the cash you need to run the business, the money you paid to purchase it will be wasted. You will have a loss-making, and therefore diminishing, asset on your hands.

Hidden costs

It is surprisingly easy to forget about the costs actually involved in making the purchase. If you have followed the advice in this book you will almost certainly have employed a solicitor to draw up the final agreement and, perhaps, to deal with matters like the assignment of leases or contracts, the drafting of vendor's warranties etc. If it is a company which you are buying then you may also have commissioned your accountants to have a pretty thorough inspection, if not a full audit, of the books and you may well have called on both solicitor and accountant for professional advice on many points. Sadly, these professional

	April	May	June	July	August	September	October	November	December	January	February	March	Totals
	£	£	£	£	£	£	£	£	£	£	£	£	£
Sales	3,500	3,500	3,500	3,500	3,500	3,500	3,500	7,000	7,000	3,500	3,500	3,500	49,000
Purchases	2,000	2,000	2,000	2,000	2,000	4,000	4,000	2,000	2,000	2,000	2,000	2,000	28,000
Rent	750	–	–	750	–	–	750	–	–	750	–	–	3,000
Rates	1,000	–	–	–	–	–	–	–	–	–	–	–	1,000
Drawings	600	600	600	600	600	600	600	600	600	600	600	600	7,200
Overheads	250	250	250	250	250	250	250	250	250	250	250	250	3,000
Total outgoings	4,600	2,850	2,850	3,600	2,850	4,850	5,600	2,850	2,850	3,600	2,850	2,850	42,200
Net income (outgoings)	(1,100)	650	650	(100)	650	(1,350)	(2,100)	4,150	4,150	(100)	650	650	6,800
Balance b/fwd	(20,000)	(21,100)	(20,450)	(19,800)	(19,900)	(19,250)	(20,600)	(22,700)	(18,550)	(14,400)	(14,500)	(13,850)	(20,000)
Balance	(21,100)	(20,450)	(19,800)	(19,900)	(19,250)	(20,600)	(22,700)	(18,550)	(14,400)	(14,500)	(13,850)	(13,200)	(13,200)

ladies and gentlemen do not offer their services for free; indeed they may value them so highly that they are currently charging £30 to £40, or more, for an hour of their time. At that rate it does not take long to run up a four figure bill. Before making a final offer and clinching the deal, therefore, it may be as well to ask for an estimate of what their charges are likely to amount to — it will be what the Americans call a 'ball park figure' but at least you will know whether you are talking about a few hundred or a few thousand pounds.

If the purchase involves the transfer of shares in a company then stamp duty will be payable on the transaction. In some circumstances, accountants can construct 'schemes' which avoid the tax, though this will require the cooperation of both parties. This is an area where proper professional advice is essential.

Your personal needs

Another very relevant factor is what you are going to draw out of the business. If you are proposing to buy a business, especially if you are moving from the position of paid employment to that of self-employment, you are in effect buying an income for yourself, your family and dependants and it is essential to establish what sort of income you need, whether the business can provide it and if the price you are paying for the business is reasonable in relation to the income it will earn. It must also be stressed that, although this chapter argues that profitability is the main yardstick for judging the value of a business, the profits of a small business may be a very different thing from money in the owner's pocket.

If, up to this point in your life, you have worked for other people and have been able to rely on a wage packet or salary cheque at regular intervals, it is tempting to assume that what you need from your new business is simply an amount equal to your current earnings, plus, perhaps, a bit extra to reward your initiative and energy. If the business you are buying is a company, this is not an unreasonable way of looking at it; you can certainly compare your requirements with the sums the previous owner was drawing by way of salary and dividends and see if they match up. But if you are buying the business of a sole trader or partnership you may not know how much the previous owner was drawing and a straight comparison between your previous earnings and your needs as a self-employed person will omit several important factors.

Tax and National Insurance

To start with you will now be taxed, not on the cash you actually receive and have available to spend, but on your profits — which may be a very different thing as we will see shortly. Secondly, you will have to buy your own National Insurance stamps, which will currently cost you £3.50 a week (Class 2 contributions) *plus* 6.3 per cent of your profits between £4150 and £13,780 (Class 4 contributions). There is, however, a ceiling on the combined total of Class 2 and Class 4 contributions of, again currently, £788 a year. But the point is made, one hopes, that having to find such sums in cash is very different from the relatively painless process of having your share of the stamp deducted on your wage slip.

Retirement

Finally, you have to think ahead to retirement. If you hope for more than the minimum state pension then you will need to consider investment in one of the many private pension schemes for the self-employed. The contributions can be a considerable burden, especially if you are no longer in the first flush of youth (and thus have a relatively short working life ahead of you during which to save for your pension). It is worth noting in this connection that, if you have previously been a member of a company pension fund, the value of the pension you have been buying will in effect, have been virtually frozen when you quit employment. This whole area is one in which it is as well to get professional advice, particularly as contributions to private pension schemes can help to offset your personal tax bill. You should also remember that, in the case of a sole trader or partnership, these costs will not show up in the accounts of the previous owners; their National Insurance contributions, tax bills and pension schemes are their own business. They may well have found the money from other sources which are not available to you.

Incidental expenses

You should be careful not to overlook, especially if you are moving out of employment into self-employment for the first time, the incidental expenses that can arise. You may, for example, be moving house; perhaps you should allow for the gap, possibly a month or two, between your last salary cheque and your first drawings from the new business. It is not the sort of item that looms large in a multi-million pound takeover bid, but at the scale on which you are working it can be far from negligible.

Negotiating

However thoroughly you have done your homework and made your assessments, sooner or later the point is going to come when you have to sit down with the vendor and actually try and strike a bargain. At this stage buying a business ceases to be an affair of calculation and becomes one of personality. It is important to remember that there will be considerations on both sides that go well beyond hard fact. For your part, you are, presumably, eager to buy, but you must not allow yourself to become too eager. A buyer who has become emotionally committed to the success of a negotiation before it has begun is in a very exposed position. For the vendor, this may be a painful as well as an exciting moment: what he is selling may be a lifetime's work and he will want to feel that it is passing into the hands of someone he can like personally who is also paying a fair price. So be prepared to meet and cope with attitudes and reactions that may seem irrational or even silly.

The way in which any negotiation is handled is so much a matter of personality that it is impossible to give any general rules which apply across the board. Approaches that may prove successful when adopted by one kind of person will be ineffectual if mimicked by someone with a different character. Perhaps the most important principle is that of knowing your own mind. This does not mean that you slap an offer on the table, snarl, 'Take it or leave it', and sit tight. It does mean that you must enter negotiations with a firm view about the business and its value to you, and not allow yourself to be swayed by your own eagerness or the vendor's arguments. Indeed, it is essential that, long before you get down to the nitty-gritty, you have foreseen and discounted the arguments he will produce, decided which are valid, from your point of view, and which are irrelevant. Ideally, nothing that he says should come as a surprise, and you should be prepared to show either how you have already taken a factor into account or why you do not feel it applies.

Opening offers

As a buyer you will almost certainly be expected to name a figure first — though in any negotiation it is an advantage to get your opponent to name one first if you can. You will naturally have decided on a limit to which you are prepared to go, but that should not be your starting point. An opening offer should be carefully calculated to fall between two extremes: it should not be so low as to be derisory, that will simply have the effect of annoying the vendor and giving an impression that you are not serious, nor should it be so high as to leave no room for manoeuvre — you must have scope for giving some ground. Remember that negotiation is a ritual. Many people will in the end accept a price which they would have turned down flat at the outset if they feel they have really fought for it and 'got you up' by dint of hard argument: allow for this factor.

Assessing the vendor's terms and attitude
At a fairly early stage you should be able to make some kind of evaluation of the man, or men, on the other side of the negotiating table. Have they got a firm target in mind? Are they looking forward to a good 'haggle' or do they find the process embarrassing and awkward? Have they marshalled their arguments and staked out the ground on which they wish to fight or can you dictate the tactics? If it becomes clear that they have a target, then try and get them to name it. This does not mean that, even if it is within your limit, you should instantly accept it, a step which might lead them to raise it, but it allows you to give ground slowly and carefully in the knowledge that you are not wasting your time. If the target is too high then, depending on how wide the gap is, you will either have to try and persuade them to come down by stages or, if the gulf is unbridgeable, perhaps try shock tactics and threaten to withdraw. In such circumstances there comes a point when one side or the other has to drastically revise its thinking. Provided that you have already reached a firm conclusion about the price you are willing to pay, you will not be persuaded to revise it — but the other side may be willing to think again (not while face to face in negotiation, though; you must give them time to regroup and rethink).

There are many people who enjoy nothing better than a long haggle over detail. However tiresome you may find this, do not try and cut the process short too abruptly. It is usually a weakness that can be exploited. By indulging them and, perhaps, conceding a minor point after long argument you will have given them the illusion of fighting a major battle at the cost of trivial casualties on your side; they may then allow a major victory to you by default. It is vital, when dealing with such opponents, to keep your mind on the main issues and not allow yourself to become bogged down in triviality; on the other hand, if the opposition want to bog themselves down, that can only be to your advantage. If, however, the vendor clearly finds detailed haggling distasteful, do not try and drag him into it unless it is really important: even if you score a point, it will be at the cost of irritating and alienating him.

Planning the discussion
The first advantage in negotiation, as in battle, goes to the side which selects the ground, or, in other words, sets the agenda. This does not mean that you should come to the negotiating table armed with numbered points for discussion, but it does mean that, if possible, you should direct the course of the discussion. Here tact is vital, as it will obviously be counter-productive to try to dictate the way things go, but if you have a clear programme in your mind, and the opposition does not, you will have a great advantage. It is well worth preparing for such an opportunity by carefully listing, even if it is only in your head, the points you want to raise and your own arguments on each of them. Do not allow yourself to be hijacked by an opponent who has made similar preparations: you may have to go through his agenda first, but it should then be possible to steer the discussion firmly round to yours.

Few negotiations will be completed in a single session. It is very important that you do not allow yourself to be bullied or cajoled into making snap decisions; if you find yourself faced with an argument or a factor which you had not anticipated, do not try and bluster or bluff your way through. Take time to think it out and consider your counter-arguments or any revision of your position that may be necessary. Nor, if your advisers — accountants or solicitors — are sitting in on the discussions should you expect them to deliver snap judgements; they, too, need time to consider. If they are not present at the negotiating table you should not reach any decision which requires their advice without gaining time in which to consult them.

Rival buyers
Perhaps the most difficult situation to cope with, as a would-be purchaser, is a competitive one where you find yourself bidding against a rival. Obviously this puts the vendors in a much stronger position, giving them a chance to play one side off

against the other. The essential thing, should you become involved in this sort of position, is to keep a clear head and remember that what you are trying to do is buy a business, not win a competition; it is surprising how easy it is to lose sight of this fact. Above all, remember that in such cases, one side has got to lose, and the losing side may well be the one that allows itself to be stampeded into paying too much. Do not be swayed by arguments, or hints, based on what your rivals are proposing: it may suit them to do things a certain way, which does not mean that it will suit you. The best policy is to try and ignore the competitive element in the situation and concentrate on what you want and how you plan to achieve it.

Conclusion
Any negotiation has a kind of natural length. At some point a stage will be reached where both sides have said all they have to say and nothing will be gained by further discussion. It is essential, at this point, to try to bring things to a head, for negotiations which drag on too long are time wasting and tiresome. Sensing when this stage has been reached is an instinctive skill which may come only with practice, but if you feel that all the arguments have been made and that neither side has anything to add, then you should try and wind things up to a firm conclusion.

Chapter 7
Paying for it

If you are in the happy position of having sufficient cash to pay for the business you are buying and meet its needs for working capital, then this chapter will be superfluous — all you have to do is write a cheque. But for most people the answer is not so simple and the buying of a business will be inextricably bound up with the problems of finding the money to pay for it which, almost inevitably, means borrowing.

Since borrowing, in turn, hinges upon the provision of security for the lender of the funds, those who provide the funds, from whatever source, will be going through, at one remove, exactly the same sort of calculations as you have made in order to decide whether the business can reasonably be expected to meet interest charges and repay principal and whether, in the last resort, the value of the assets gives adequate cover. Thus if you have deluded yourself with over-optimism, you can expect to be brought down to earth swiftly by your backers or bank manager.

However you hope to borrow, and whomever you hope to borrow from, the basic equipment you will need is the same. A lender will want to see the past accounts of the business, together with the gloss you have placed on them in the shape of your own valuation of the assets and your forecasts of future profitability and cash flow and, of course, your plans for developing and improving the business. If you are planning to combine the new business with an existing one, then you will have to show the figures for the two enterprises combined.

If you are starting your search for funds from scratch, so to speak, without any support other than your own savings and skills, your first port of call almost certainly will be one of the big four clearing banks. Between them the High Street banks are far and away the largest, and in many ways the most convenient, source of finance for small businesses. All other things being equal, you will probably go to the branch which already has your private or business account. But it is as well to remember that the banks are in competition with each other and it does not follow that, because a proposal is turned down by one, it will be turned down by all. On the other hand, managers operate within fairly narrow guidelines and on very similar principles, and it is certainly futile to expect that even the most helpful of them will abandon caution and take a flyer — bank managers can be distressingly earthbound men.

Overdrafts

The simplest way of borrowing from a bank is a straightforward overdraft facility, an agreement that you can go into the red up to an agreed limit. This has the great advantage of flexibility; at any given moment you are borrowing and paying for only what you need. It has the disadvantage, first, that you will be paying interest at the top end of the range and that the rate will vary with the bank's 'base rate' and therefore cannot be forecast with any accuracy. An overdraft limit that looked perfectly workable when base rate was 10 per cent looks like a nightmare when it rises to 15. Second, a bank can, in principle, withdraw an overdraft facility at its own discretion. Obviously, few banks will want to actually slam the door unless things look very bad indeed; but even if a business is going well external factors — a government credit squeeze, a change in bank policy or even a new manager — can lead to pressure on a business to reduce its borrowings to a lower limit. From the bank's point of view, an overdraft is the most risky form of lending it can indulge in and the one that gives it the least freedom to plan ahead; even if you are well within your limit, the bank has to assume that you may need to use it to the full at any time.

Any bank manager who is asked to provide funds on overdraft for the purchase of a business will want to be satisfied on three basic points. First, can the business be expected to generate sufficient profits to pay the interest charges and reduce the borrowing steadily in the short- to medium-term future? Second, has the borrower himself got a substantial stake in the business? Normally, a bank will not be willing to provide finance on overdraft unless the borrower is matching its risk with an investment on his own account. A ratio of owner's funds to bank borrowing of between 1:1 and 1:2 is the sort of figure the bank would consider reasonable.

Finally, a bank will expect to have some form of security. If a business has substantial assets, such as property, which are freely saleable, then these may be considered adequate but, if the business is to be organised as a sole trader or a partnership you must remember that, in the last resort, all your personal assets are at risk. The bank may, indeed, want to formalise this aspect of affairs by, for example, having a mortgage on your house as well as the business premises. In the case of a company, where the status of limited liability leaves the bank more 'exposed' and the shareholders less so, you may find that the bank will require personal guarantees from shareholders or directors which effectively waive the limited liability.

Loans

An alternative to the simple overdraft which may be preferable for both bank and customer is a short- or medium-term loan. Most banks have a variety of loan schemes tailored to the needs of small businesses or even, in cases such as agriculture, to the requirements of a particular kind of business. It will, therefore, pay to shop around and see which scheme might best suit your requirements. The principles, however, will be very similar.

The bank undertakes to lend a fixed sum at a fixed rate of interest and the customer undertakes to pay the interest at regular intervals and to repay the capital in set instalments over an agreed period. A typical example might be a loan of £20,000 at an interest rate of, say, 12½ per cent repayable in five annual instalments of £4000, the first repayment becoming due three years after the start of the loan period. Some schemes seek to help the customer by fixing a much lower rate of interest, say 7½ per cent, which is payable on the whole amount over the whole period of the loan. This has the effect of lowering the interest charges in the first few years and transferring the burden to the later ones when, it is assumed, the benefits of the loan will enable the business to bear them. In the case of the example quoted, the borrower would be paying only 7½ per cent for his money at the start, but in the final year of the loan he would be paying 7½ per cent of £20,000 for a loan which had been reduced to only £4000. The banks will, of course, show you tables which indicate the true, averaged rate of interest that loans of this sort involve.

The advantages of a loan as opposed to an overdraft are essentially those of predictability: you know how much money you will have available, for how long and on what terms. The disadvantages boil down to a lack of flexibility, especially when it comes to repayments which have to be made as and when due, which can prove awkward if, as is the nature of any business, things do not go completely according to plan.

It should be obvious from what has been said that, while borrowing from a bank will almost certainly be the best source of working capital and may be a suitable way of 'topping up' your own resources when purchasing a business, it is not the best way of finding the kind of long-term capital that may be required if the gap between the cash you have available and the price you have to pay for an acquisition is a large one. The clearing banks, in short, are not in the business of providing funds which may have to remain invested in a business for a long period.

However, it should be borne in mind that almost all the major clearing banks have, in recent years, set up affiliated organisations whose purpose is to provide venture capital for the small- to medium-sized business. Your local bank manager will be acquainted with his bank's investment schemes and will be able to provide you with literature and information about them.

We shall look at other financial institutions which may provide a source of capital in a moment, but the sort of help they can offer is, in general, restricted to companies, where the ownership and management of a business can be easily and conveniently divided, which is not the case with sole traders or partnerships.

Private sources of capital

An individual who needs capital to buy a business and who cannot, or does not wish to, get it from his bank has only two resources: to borrow privately or to find a partner, either active or sleeping. Many people do of course mortgage their houses, even pawn belongings and otherwise stake their entire savings on buying a business — and succeed. But, before taking the plunge, it is as well to remember that those you hear about are the ones that succeed; no one has space to report the sorry tales of those who gamble and lose.

There is, alas, no set procedure or system for putting those who seek a partner with money to spare in touch with those who need them. It is, quite simply, a matter of luck and personal contacts. There is, however, a very basic rule to remember should you be fortunate enough to find such a person who is willing to risk his or her money by backing your talent: put the arrangement in writing. Partnership law is complicated and it is vital that both parties know where they stand, what their rights and obligations are and, most importantly, how power and responsibility are allocated between them. A partnership agreement will spell such matters out and, remember, the main purpose of any agreement is to determine what happens when things go wrong — when things go right it is probably not needed. So do not be afraid or embarrassed, but insist that the nitty-gritty is there in black and white to be referred to if the worst should happen.

This is especially important in the case of sleeping partners, for the interests of the sleeping partner may be very different from those of his working colleague. It is, for example, all too easy to arrive at a situation where, having quit paid employment in order to have the freedom of working for yourself, you find that you are, in effect, simply working for your sleeping partner who, because he holds the purse strings, calls the tune. If you like each other and your minds work along the same lines, this may be fine; but what happens if, God forbid, he dies, or you quarrel, or he falls on hard times and needs his money for other purposes? In the absence of a proper partnership agreement which makes provision for such eventualities you may find your relationship abruptly dissolved and the business you have so laboriously cared for put up for sale.

But you may be fortunate enough to be able to borrow privately without resorting either to taking on a partner or mortgaging your house or other private possessions. If you have a well-to-do friend or relation it may be worthwhile approaching them for a loan; since they will know you well, they may be willing to lend you money without demanding security and may in fact settle for a lower rate of interest. An alternative would be to ask your friend or relation personally to guarantee a bank overdraft for your business. But whatever arrangement you make, be sure to have it in writing; in fact, you should go one step further and have any written agreement vetted and approved by your solicitor. This is particularly important if the person involved is elderly; his or her death, unless its eventuality is covered in writing, could mean financial ruin for you if the estate calls in the loan.

Venture capital

A limited company can spread its net much wider in the search for capital, not only because it is likely to be a larger and more established business than a sole trader or partnership, but also because there are clearly defined ways in which its control and ownership can be divided, and because, as a business, it has an identity and a continuity which go beyond those of its owners.

If you are buying a company and need to raise cash to pay for it and your High Street bank is not an appropriate source, you will be looking at two options, or a combination of them: selling some proportion of the shareholding or obtaining long-term loan capital.

From your point of view, diluting your ownership of the business by allowing others to hold shares in it is something to be avoided as far as possible. Not only are you thereby giving them a voice in the way the business is run, but you are also granting them a share of your profit, whether it takes the shape of a dividend cheque or an increase in the value of the business. For precisely those reasons, however, it is more than likely that a share in the business will be the price which anyone demands in exchange for their financial help.

Loan capital, usually in the form of a debenture, is almost always preferable. A debenture usually takes the form of a loan for a fixed term at a fixed rate of interest. It differs from the sort of loan that a bank will offer in so far as it normally runs for a longer period and is repayable in one fell swoop at the end of that period rather than in instalments. Interest, as with a bank loan, will have to be paid come what may, and the debenture holder's security lies in the fact that he has preference over every other creditor should the company go into liquidation (it is, of course, for this reason that a debenture holder has the right to appoint a receiver and wind up a company which is running into trouble).

In practice, raising capital from most sources will boil down to some combination of these two methods and the trick is to negotiate the one which gives you the capital you require while conceding the smallest share of the company's equity you can manage. Within these broad limits, the two figures that should be in the back of your mind are 51 and 76. The owner of 51 per cent of a company's voting shares has effective control of it, and the owner of 76 per cent has total control — that is, he can, within the law, enforce his wishes against those of other shareholders. For the small businessman, the commonest sources of this kind of capital will be one or another of the organisations which provide venture capital; a complete list of these, compiled by the *Investors Chronicle*, is given on pages 120-43. As can be seen, they include offshoots of the major clearing banks, merchant banks, funds organised by stockbrokers or the financial institutions and businesses, like Investors in Industry, which have been set up explicitly to meet this need. The sort of propositions each is prepared to consider vary widely; some for example exist entirely to offer their fund-holders the chance to benefit from the tax concessions available to investors via the Business Expansion Scheme (see page 116); others are primarily interested in building businesses up prior to launching them on to the Unlisted Securities Market, while others may concentrate on particular sectors of business or particular geographical areas.

Given that few of them will make a snap investment decision, and given that, from your point of view, time is likely to be at a premium, you will probably find it best to draw up a formal proposal showing what you need the money for, how much is required and how you propose to repay it, and circulate to a number of institutions simultaneously. At this first stage, you do not need to make any concrete proposals as to how much of the money would be invested by way of a purchase of shares and how much by way of loan capital; individual institutions may have different preferences about this, and you can, in preparing your figures, treat the whole amount as borrowing and explain that you will, of course, be ready to negotiate an equity stake should things go a stage further.

The exact form such a proposal takes will vary from case to case, but the sort of ground it should cover is really a matter of common sense. Any potential investor will want to know as much as possible about the business you are buying, your own track record, your qualifications for running it and, of course, your forecasts of profit and cash flow. If substantial assets are involved, such as property, it may also be useful to obtain an independent valuation and attach it.

Preparing such a proposal will involve you in a lot of work, and in some cases, institutions may insist that you fit the financial forecasts into a standard formula of their own devising. You will very likely need the help of an accountant, and you may be able to find an accountant, or some other individual with the right contacts and expertise (a stockbroker, for example) who is prepared to act as middleman and make approaches on your behalf. An accountant will charge for his services whatever happens; his professional body will not allow him to accept payment by results, but others may undertake to raise capital in return for a finder's fee or commission, usually something like 2 to 3 per cent of the sum raised. You should be sure, before entering into such an arrangement, that you understand what is involved and the terms that have been agreed.

Government schemes to help small businesses

It may be worth your while to investigate the many sources of financial aid to small businesses which both local and central government offer. The range of such schemes is wide and includes government-guaranteed overdrafts, subsidised rates and rent in certain areas, and loans to allow you to purchase new equipment.

Currently, the most significant source of government help, albeit indirect, is the Business Expansion Scheme. This is designed to stimulate investment in new or growing businesses whose shares cannot be traded on the open market. It allows investors to offset such investment against their personal tax liabilities, up to a total, currently, of £40,000 in any one year. The concession is available to the individual investor (though a minimum investment of £500 is required) and can, therefore, be a valuable incentive to a person with some cash to spare who wishes to back a small business such as the one you are intending to buy. There are rules and conditions of course, but they are not onerous and your Inspector of Taxes will be able to supply you with full details if you want to check that an investment in your business will qualify for the concession.

But, so far at least, the vast bulk of the qualifying investment has been handled through funds set up for the purpose and, rather disappointingly, the majority of these are not equipped to look after the needs of the relatively small businessman looking for, perhaps £20,000 or £30,000 at the maximum. There are, however, exceptions to this rule, especially where funds have been set up to encourage job creation in one particular locality, so it is well worth investigating the possibilities.

If your own small business has a good track record and you wish to expand it by the purchase of another, you may stand a good chance of obtaining a small business loan guarantee from the government. Under this arrangement, the government guarantees a loan (part of which is usually an overdraft) through your local bank based on its assessment of your future profitability. The ceiling for such a loan usually goes up in each year's central government budget. You will be asked by your bank to prepare detailed financial forecasts for your business and, if it approves of these, it will seek government help on your behalf. However, this scheme has not been guaranteed beyond December 1985.

Is the business you want to buy in a redevelopment area? If so, and if it has a work force, then you stand a good chance of receiving grants or help with the rates or rent. If you feel that, with your improved management of the new firm and the purchase of new machinery, you will actually be in a position to increase the work force, then you stand an excellent chance of receiving a grant, a subsidy, or a loan from either central or local government. This is particularly true if you live in an area of high unemployment.

Finding out about help from government or quasi-government sources can involve you in a great deal of investigation, but those who eventually benefit from it reckon their efforts to have been well worthwhile. Again, your bank manager is a good person to start with and he can at least point you in the right direction in your search for government funding. The Department of Trade and Industry issues literature concerning government help for small business; and, if your company has employees, it is worth telephoning the Manpower Services Commission, which has developed a number of schemes to help small businesses increase their work forces. Since you will most likely be dealing with your local authority over a number of issues such as planning permission and rates, do ask them about any schemes they might have for helping small businesses raise venture capital.

Making the business buy itself

One final source of cash is the business itself. If there is some part, or aspect, of it which can be hived off and sold as a separate entity, or if it can be moved to a new location or combined with an existing business under one roof, thus releasing property which can be sold, this may well be a quick and relatively painless way of finding cash. But it is vital to be realistic about this kind of possibility; in the case of many businesses it is, quite simply, not an option because there is nothing that can be sold without damaging the organisation.

For example, while it may be entirely reasonable to sell the High Street premises of, say, a builders merchant and move it to a less valuable site, the same decision would destroy within weeks a shop which relies upon a passing retail trade.

You will also have to take into account that, in virtually every instance, selling some part of a business will reduce its size and, thus, its ability to generate profit. Before settling on any such plan it is important to make sure that you have analysed the performance of the various parts of a business and the way that they interrelate. Suppose, for instance, that you are buying a bakery that has both a retail shop and a contract business supplying other shops with bread, pastries etc. It is not enough simply to calculate that the shop makes a higher profit and that the contract business can be sold off to a competitor, for the fact that the shop is extremely profitable may be due to the economies of scale the bakery obtains by producing large quantities, and that both shop and bakery would be uneconomic without the contracts with other shops. The reverse may equally well apply; the fact that there is a demand for the produce in other outlets may be in large part due to the reputation of the shop; or that it would be impossible to supply produce to others at such competitive prices if the retail business was not there to help spread costs. In other words, it is rash to assume that a business can be divided into its constituent parts without damaging all of them to some degree.

If you are contemplating the possibility of dismembering a business which has more than one aspect to it in order to pay for, and concentrate on, the part which you wish to keep, it is as well to understand the two basic ways in which aspects of a business are integrated — what business schools call the vertical and the horizontal. We are, by the way, ignoring the once-fashionable 'conglomerate' structure which simply lumped totally disparate businesses together under one roof; this is not an arrangement which is common in small businesses, and it is easy enough to take such a structure apart; indeed, it will fall apart unaided in most cases.

A business which has grown 'vertically' has taken advantage of the fact that most trades are in fact a hierarchy of specialised businesses, each handling the goods or product at one stage of its journey to the market place. The commonest examples would, perhaps, be manufacture, wholesale and retail. Obviously, a business which short-circuits the chain and thus cuts out one middleman, and his profit, will have advantages over a competitor who handles only one stage. It is simple enough to see that if a business has been put together on this principle it can be dismantled again to leave two or more businesses, each concentrating on a single level. But it must be borne in mind that such a step is likely to leave parts which are less competitive than the whole, and more dependent upon suppliers at the next level up, or customers at the next level down.

A business which has expanded horizontally, in contrast, has spread from one particular product or range of activities into other neighbouring or related ones. The rationale, apart from growth, is likely to have been that many costs or services — sales effort, perhaps, or a distribution system — could be shared; so, again, it cannot be assumed that the businesses that have been combined on this basis can be separated painlessly without affecting the efficiency or profitability of either.

Deciding how to split up a business clearly depends on being able to identify the true costs and income of each constituent part (each profit centre, as business jargon has it) and, in particular, the needs of each part for working capital. Obviously, since you are considering dividing the business in order to raise money, the ideal solution is to keep those parts which are most profitable, but to balance this objective against your need to reduce the calls on the working capital as far as possible. Unless the points at which the various aspects of the business are welded together are obvious, or form natural fissures, it will be best to take your time over this critical process and make sure that you fully understand the implications of every possible step.

SOURCES OF FINANCE

A guide to development and venture capital facilities

Vehicle for capital	Backers	Capital earmarked	Type of Client or situation	Min/max funds injected	Start up capital
Abingworth plc Tel: (01) 839 6745	Listed authorised investment trust	Open	Companies with high growth prospects, principally in high technology	£100,000 – £500,000 and occasionally larger amounts	Yes, if management of proven calibre
Advent Ltd Tel: (01) 630 9811 (0534) 75151	Financial institutions, corporations and universities	£60m in three funds	High growth companies exploiting new technology	£100,000 – £1·5m	Yes
Alta Berkeley Associates Tel: (01) 629 1550	International institutions, corporations and universities	£30m	Technology companies	£100,000 – £1m	Yes, if management is proven
APA Ventures II Tel: (01) 493 3633	Alan Patricof Associates	£40m	Companies with high growth prospects, management buy-outs	£100,000 – £3m	Yes
ASSET: Ardrossan, Saltcoats, Stevenston Enterprise Trust Tel: Saltcoats (0294) 602515/6	Scottish Development Agency Strathclyde Regional Council Clydesdale Bank plc	£150,000	New businesses to create employment	£1,000 – £5,000	Yes
Avon Enterprise Fund plc Tel: (0272) 213206	Institutions primarily associated with the West of England	£1·5m initially	Companies with proven management and good growth potential	£25,000 – £150,000. Larger requirements can be syndicated	Yes, for proven management with a fully developed product/service
Baker Street Investment Company plc (BASIC) Tel: (01) 486 5021	Leading UK institutions	£5m	Proven management. Good growth potential	£100,000 – £400,000	In exceptional circumstances
Barclays Development Capital Tel: (01) 623 4321	Barclays Bank Group	Open	Established growth companies earning £100,000+ pre-tax	£150,000 minimum. No maximum but may syndicate	No
Baring Brothers Hambrecht & Quist Tel: (01) 626 5133	Financial institutions, corporations and individuals	Over £20m	Balanced portfolio from start-ups to management buy-outs	£100,000 – £1m	Yes

Where to go when the bank manager says 'no'.

Rescue capital	Equity stake	Seat on board	Term of funding	Exit criteria	Special features	Portfolio
Occasionally	Always minority	Usually	Open	Flexible, but happy to take long term view	Extensive overseas contacts — US, Europe and the Far East	£60m+ in the UK and US
Occasionally	Significant minority	Yes	Flexible	Flexible	Help to companies. International network of venture capital funds	£20m in 40 companies
Possibly	Minority	Usually	Open	Flexible	Affiliated with US venture capital company. Contacts in US and continent	Founded 1983
Yes	Minority equity investments	Yes	Approx 5 years	Generally USM or other market listing	Presence in New York & Paris. High and low-tech. Active help to companies	£7·4m in 24 companies
No	Nil	No	1 to 5 years	—	Special loan funds available. 16/25 years — £100,000	53 businesses started through our Loan Scheme
No	Yes, normally in the range of 20-40%	Reserve the right but do not often exercise it	Open	No set criteria	Invests mainly in Avon, Gloucester-shire, Somerset and Wiltshire	Fund established in July 1984 — 2 investments
No	Yes, minority	Yes, in participating non-executive capacity	5 years upwards	As seems appropriate	Management support provided	11 companies – £2·6m
Exceptionally	Yes — 10-40%	Usually	Open	Flexible	Able to formulate equity/loan packages in co-operation with Barclays branches	43 companies – £22m
Unlikely	Always minority	Where appropriate	Up to 10 years	Flexible	Strong international presence — affiliated funds in US and Japan	6 investments — £2·5m

This table is reproduced by kind permission of *Investors Chronicle*.

Baronsmead Associates Limited Tel: (01) 638 6826	Newmarket (Venture Capital)	None. It is arranged as needed on a syndicated basis	High growth technology bias. Particularly interested in start-ups	£100,000 upwards	Yes	Possibly
Biotechnology Investments Limited Tel: (01) 280 5000	NM Rothschild and leading UK institutions	$85m	Biotechnology companies worldwide at all stages of development	Flexible; but generally $500,000 – $2m; would syndicate	Yes	Occasionally
Birmingham Technology Ltd Tel: Birmingham (021) 359 0981	Lloyds Bank plc Birmingham City Council University of Aston	£5m to be augmented as and when needed	Hi-tech research, development and/or high-tech assembly companies	£20,000 – £300,000. Would syndicate larger sums	Yes	Possibly
Britannia Development Capital Limited Tel: (01) 588 2777	Britannia Arrow Holdings plc	Open	Quality unquoted companies. Good management and growth prospects are key	Min £100,000. Syndicates arranged where necessary	Possible	Possible
British Rail Pension Funds Tel: (01) 247 7600	—	Open	Established business and management	£100,000 – £750,000	No	Rarely
British Technology Group (BTG) Tel: (01) 403 6666	HM Government	Open	Finance for the development and exploitation of new technology	No fixed limits	Yes	No
Brown Shipley Developments Tel: (01) 606 9833	Brown Shipley & Co	Open	Quality of individuals of prime importance and above average growth sectors	£50,000 minimum preference shares, may syndicate and provide loans	No	Exceptionally
Cambium Venture Capital plc Tel: (01) 628 5070	Publicly quoted company	£2m	Technology content, leisure	£50,000 – £300,000	Yes	Yes
Candover Investments plc Tel: (01) 583 5090	7 leading UK institutions	Open	Management buy-outs and conventional development capital situations	£2m+	No	No
Castle Finance Tel: Norwich (0603) 22200	Norwich Union Insurance Group	Open	Profitable private companies requiring capital for expansion	£100,000 – £1m. Larger amounts considered	Exceptionally	No

Yes	Yes	Medium/long term	Look for commitment to sell or public market	Specialist in syndicated start-ups	Manages £12m in 27 companies
Up to 20% exceptionally higher	Normally	Flexible	Flexible; flotation preferred but aim to be long-term investors	Active management support. Experience in USA. Team of scientific consultants	$30m in 25 companies
Yes	Yes	Flexible according to requirements	Flexible	Exclusively hi-tech related enterprise	7 companies — £720,000
Yes	Normally	No prescribed limit	Flexible but flotation preferred	Innovative approach. Complementary corporate advisory services. Close rapport with management	10 BES investments 32 other investments
Up to 49%	Right usually sought	Up to 7 years	Flotations, sale, redemption	Further funding always available in appropriate cases	£23m
If appropriate	If appropriate	Finance provided in the form of project finance, or equity if appropriate	Flexible	Will also invest in projects with larger companies	About 250 projects and investments with total book value of £30m
Yes, usually 10-30%	Frequently in active non-executive capacity	Equity: open Loans: up to 8 years	Flotation or sale or require running yield	Other merchant banking facilities available. Aim to establish a close relationship	32 companies
Yes	Yes	Up to 5 years	Stock market flotation or management buy-out	—	—
Always minority	Yes	Open	Flexible	Investment arranged through syndicate of shareholders and possibly other investors	£150m invested in 45 companies in UK and US
Normally up to 30%	No	Flexible to suit each situation	Looking for dividends: sale of equity when convenient to all	Supplementary financial services of the Norwich Union Insurance Group	Currently 25 companies. Total money invested to date: £12·5m

Vehicle for capital	Backers	Capital earmarked	Type of Client or situation	Min/max funds injected	Start up capital	Rescue capital
Causeway Development Capital Fund Tel: (01) 631 3073	Major pension funds	£10·6m	Growing companies, management buy-outs, etc	£400,000 – £1m	Selectively	Selectively
Charterhouse Development Tel: (01) 248 4000	Charterhouse J Rothschild	Not disclosed	Companies of above average quality, ie with good growing earnings	£100,000 – £5m	Rarely	No
Charterhouse Japhet Venture Fund Tel: (01) 409 3232	UK pension funds	£16·5m	Young companies with high growth opportunities, management buy-outs, usually high-tech	£200,000 – £1m	Yes, including seed capital	Unlikely
CIN Industrial Finance Tel: (01) 629 6000	National Coal Board Pension Funds	£45m — £50m per annum	Small and medium sized private companies with growth potential	£250,000 – £5m	Yes, but very selective	Yes, viable subsidiaries or divisions
Citicorp Venture Capital Tel: (01) 438 1593/ 1271	Citicorp	Not capital constrained	Replacement expansion and start-up capital	£250,000 min, no max	Sometimes, depending on good management and prospects	Exceptionally
Close Investment Management Tel: (01) 283 2244	8 major insurance companies and pension funds	£30m	Small and medium sized UK companies	Minimum £100,000 no maximum but may syndicate over £2m	Exceptionally	Possibly
Clydesdale Bank Equity Ltd Tel: Glasgow (041) 248 7070	Clydesdale Bank/Midland Bank	£5m	Profitable private companies with potential for growth	Normally £100,000+ but will consider proposals at lower level	Yes — highly selective	Exceptionally — would consider backing new management
Colonnade Development Capital plc Tel: (01) 638 2575	Bown Goldie & Co Savory Milln	£4·25m	Development capital	£250,000+	No	No
Commonwealth Development Finance Company Ltd Tel: (01) 407 9711	Several Commonwealth central banks and 140 major UK companies	£30m or equivalent in foreign exchange	Proven management and profit record, preferably seeking funds for expansion	£250,000 – £2m	No	No
Council for Small Industries in Rural Areas (CoSIRA) Tel: Salisbury (0722) 336255	HM Government plus financial institutions including ICFC under new scheme	£20m	Companies with under 20 skilled employees in countryside or small towns	£250 – £75,000 or maximum ⅓ or ½ of project cost	Loans are available for new starters	No

Equity stake	Seat on board	Term of funding	Exit criteria	Special features	Portfolio
10-49%	Usually	According to project need	Seek exit at appropriate time	Larger amounts by syndication. Active help for management	New funds. Expect about 10 investments by end March
Yes	Yes	Open	To suit company and shareholders	Non-executive director advising and helping the company	Over 125 companies — £100m in unlisted companies
Less than 50%	Yes	3-8 years	Flexible but usually flotation or sale	Positive contribution to management	8 companies — £4m
Yes, 10-49%	Yes, when a significant stake is taken	Medium and long-term loans with equity participation	Flexible to suit the company and the shareholders	Support given for acquisitions; developments. Close relationship with senior management	£200m in 140 companies
Yes	Yes	Open	Open, flotation or sale preferred	Fast response. Access to international network of Citicorp	Over £18m in 30 companies in UK. Over $170m in 127 companies in US
Yes — 10-40%	When appropriate	Medium to long term	Flexible	Continuing financial advice/ banking finance from Close Brothers Group	Investments in 25 companies
Normally 20-40%	Takes the right to appoint a director	Open	Running yield with sale when convenient to majority shareholders	Flexibility	8 companies — £1,158,000
Yes	Usually	n/a	Within 5 years	—	—
Yes, 10-45%	In most cases	Up to 10 years	Through local flotation or sale to partners. Looks for dividends	Highly flexible as to form of equity financing	40 worldwide investments — £25m
No	No	Building loans — 20 years. Equipment loans — 5 years	Repayment of loan	Availability of long-term building loans. Local representatives throughout the country	2,500 "live" loans — £19m committed

Vehicle for capital	Backers	Capital earmarked	Type of Client or situation	Min/max funds injected	Start up capital
County Bank Development Capital Tel: (01) 638 6000	National Westminster Bank	Open	Any growth company with proven management	£200,000+ sometimes less	Possibly
Darnaway Venture Capital plc Tel: Edinburgh (031) 225 9677	TSB Scotland FS Assurance Lothian Region ECI Raeburn Investment Trust	£1·5m	Venture capital for all industries, mainly in Scotland	£25,000 – £1·n	Yes
Development Capital Group Ltd Tel: (01) 486 5021	Leading UK institutions	Open	Proven management. Minimum £100,000 pre-tax profit potential	£150,000 – £2m or more through syndication	Yes, under certain circumstances
East Anglian Securities Trust Limited Tel: (0603) 660931 (0473) 213237	Institutional shareholders and private investment clients	Open	Development capital, start-ups and management buy-outs	£50,000+	Yes, if management has expertise
East of Scotland Industrial Investments plc Tel: (031) 226 4421	Leading UK institutions	£11m	Established profitable companies	£50,000 – £750,000	Occasionally, if proven management e.g. in a management buy-out
East of Scotland Onshore plc Tel: (031) 226 4421	Leading UK institutior s	£7m	Established companies — the oil service sector	£50,000 – £500,000	Occasionally if proven management
Electra Investment Trust plc Tel: (01) 836 7766	—	Currently over £100m invested in unlisted companies	Broad range	£500,000 – £3m	Occasionally
English & Caledonian plc Tel: (01) 626 7197 (01) 283 3531	Clients of Gartmore Investment, Edinburgh Investment Trust and other investors	Initially £5m	Private companies able to obtain a listing within 5 years	£200,000 – £750,000. Larger sums can be syndicated	Yes, if management has previous experience in similar markets
Equity Capital for Industry Tel: (01) 606 1000	City institutions	£50m	Companies with growth potential — not financial services or property	£100,000 – £1m	Yes

Rescue capital	Equity stake	Seat on board	Term of funding	Exit criteria	Special features	Portfolio
Exceptionally	If appropriate often 10-15% usually less than 25%	Usually ask for the right but rarely exercise it	Loans up to 20 years: equity open	No set criteria — whenever it suits the company and its shareholders	Full range merchant banking services including advice on financial matters	Over £80m in equity linked funding to 170 companies
Yes	Yes	Yes	Long-term	No stipulation	Hands-on assistance. Industrial experience	—
Yes	Yes, minority	Yes, in participating non-executive capacity	5 years upwards	As appropriate	Management supprt provided	50-60 companies — £30m
Occasionally	Small minority	Occasionally	—	Market for shares in whatever form appropriate	Personal financial commitment of executives normally expected	16 investments all UK based
Exceptionally	Yes, always minority	Yes	Equity and long-term loan capital, as a package	Open	Formulate financial package. Supplementary financial advice, close relationship with management	13 companies — £3·9m
Occasionally	Yes, always minority	Yes	Equity and long-term loan capital as a package	Open	Formulate financial package. Supplementary financial advice, close relationship with management	16 companies — £5m
Yes	Yes	Flexible	Equity based	Sought in 5-7 years	—	Over £100m invested in unlisted companies — about 50% in US
Yes, if new management or management buy-out	Yes, 10-49%	Yes	—	Flexible. Aim to capitalise by flotation	Do not necessarily require dividend on equity stake	12 companies — £6m invested
Selectively	5-45%	Usually	Long-term: equity/ convertible loan package; tailored to circumstances	Flexible	Long-term relationship with active support	55 companies — £40m invested

Vehicle for capital	Backers	Capital earmarked	Type of Client or situation	Min/max funds injected	Start up capital
European Investment Bank *Tel:* *(01) 222 2933*	European Economic Community	Over £70m for loans only at end-1984	Small and medium-sized venture in industry, tourism and related services	Maximum contribution is 50% of fixed asset cost of project	n/a
First Welsh General Investment Trust Limited *Tel: Cardiff (0222) 396131*	Commercial Bank of Wales plc	£100,000 initially	Management buy-out and any company with a short trading record	Subject to negotiation	In certain circumstances
Fleming Ventures Ltd *Tel:* *(01) 638 5858*	Robert Fleming & Co	£15m	Early stage and start up	£200,000 – £1m	Yes
Fountain Development Capital Fund *Tel:* *(01) 628 8011*	Hill Samuel, pension funds and insurance companies	£7m	Any company with two years trading record	£100,000 – £750,000	No
Gartmore Investment Trusts *Tel:* *(01) 623 1212*	Gartmore Investment Management Ltd	Open	Venture capital, management buy-outs, special situations, and development capital	£250,000 – £10m	Yes
Granville Venture Capital Fund *Tel:* *(01) 621 1212*	British Gas Pension Fund, South Yorkshire CCS Fund, The Monks Investment Trust, Confederation Life Insurance Co.	£10m	Young companies requiring funds for growth	£100,000 – £1m	Yes
Greater London Enterprise Board *Tel:* *(01) 403 0300*	Greater London Council	£25m	Manufacturing companies with 40+ in workforce as general rule	Up to £1m but higher in exceptional circumstances	Yes
Gresham Trust *Tel:* *(01) 606 6474*	Subsidiary of Eagle Star Insurance Co Ltd	Open	Profitable private companies seeking expansion, realisations or management buy-outs	£50,000 – £750,000. Will syndicate larger amounts	Where experience and track record
Grosvenor Development Capital Ltd *Tel: Slough (0753) 32623*	British Rail Pension Fund, County Bank, ECI, BTG	£10m	Development situations. Management buy-outs	£100,000 – £700,000	No

Rescue capital	Equity stake	Seat on board	Term of funding	Exit criteria	Special features	Portfolio
n/a	No	No	8-10 years including 2 year capital repayment moratorium	n/a	Priority to small and medium sized companies. Government covers exchange risk.	Over 400 ventures backed between 1973 and 1984
No	Yes and/or option — not essential	Possibly by nominees — not essential	Up to 10 years	By negotiation	None	—
No	Yes	Yes	5 years	USM or equivalent public listing or sale	Market focus in electronic components and equipment, semi-conductors. tele-communica-tions	2 investments
No	Always minority	Yes	Equity and/or loan	Open	Availability of merchant bank services and other specialist management assistance	UK only
No	Yes	Yes	—	Flotation, merger, acquisition	—	—
No	15-49%	Yes	Long-term capital	Flotation	Active support in developing/ implementing client business plans	£4m in 12 companies
Yes	As necessary	As necessary	Flexible	Flexible	Investment linked to employment creation/ protection in GLC area	—
Exceptionally	Usually, but always a minority holding	Yes	Preference shares or loans: 5-10 years. Equity: open	Running yield with sale only when sought by major shareholders	Gresham director on board. Full range of merchant banking services	60 companies — £6m
No	Yes, usually 20-40%	Yes	Long-term equity or convertible loan package	Flexible	Able to contribute financial and general management skills	22 companies — £7·1m

129

Vehicle for capital	Backers	Capital earmarked	Type of Client or situation	Min/max funds injected	Start up capital	Rescue capital
Growth Options Limited (contact through NatWest Branch) *Tel: (01) 628 9888*	Subsidiary of National Westminster Bank plc	Open	Companies with good growth potential, sound management with progressive outlook	£10,000 – £100,000	Yes	No except for management buy-outs
The Guidehouse Group plc *Tel: (01) 606 6321*	Public	Open	Flexible — syndicated purchases, management buy-outs, venture or development capital	Up to £200,000 directly	Yes	Yes
Hafren Investment Finance Ltd *Tel: Cardiff (0222) 32955*	Welsh Development Agency	£2m	High growth operations	£10,000 – £200,000	Yes	No
Hambro International Venture Fund *Tel: (01) 588 2851*	Various	$50·5m	Growth companies	$200,000 – $500,000	Yes	Yes
Hambros Advanced Technology Trust *Tel: (01) 588 2851*	Hambros Bank	£5m	Technology industries. High growth	£100,000 – £500,000	Yes	Yes
Highlands and Islands Development Board *Tel: Inverness (0463) 234171*	HM Government (Scottish Office)	£17·5m	Mainly manufacturing, tourist, agriculture, fisheries in the Scottish Highlands and Islands	Up to £400,000	Yes	Yes
Hoare Candover Exempt Fund *Tel: (01) 583 5090*	25 pension funds and charities	£7·35m	Principally management buy-outs	Minimum £250,000	No	No
ICFC *Tel: (01) 928 7822*	Investors in Industry (nine clearing banks and the Bank of England)	Unlimited	Small and medium sized companies, public and private	Up to £2m	Yes	Exceptionally
3i Ventures *Tel: (01) 928 7822*	Investors in Industry plc	Unlimited	High growth, high technology, new and young companies	£200,000 – £2m	Yes	Possibly
Innotech Limited *Tel: (01) 834 2492*	Private individuals	Open	Fast growing small to medium sized companies in higher technology	£100,000 – £500,000	Exceptionally	Rarely

Equity stake	Seat on board	Term of funding	Exit criteria	Special features	Portfolio
Option taken to subscribe for minority shareholding — usually under 25%	Right retained for board representation but not normally exercised	Up to 10 years, with holiday repayment period available	Judged on individual basis	Finance provided in form of unsecured subordinated loan	80 companies
Preferably yes, but flexible, eg, royalty income	If required	Open and flexible	Tailored to be realistic	Corporate financial, acquisition and disposal advice, lease and HP finance	Company and partners — approx £0·5m in around 10 companies
Yes, up to 30%	Yes	Open	Flexible	Advisory services	13 companies — £810,000
Yes	Usually	Variable	Public offering/ sale of company		29 companies
Yes	Usually	Open	Public offering/ sale of company	Advice & support. Full range of merchant banking services. Good links in US	17 companies
Up to 40%	Exceptionally	5-10 years. 20 years for building loans	Equity by sale	Supplementary advisory and support services	6,500 businesses assisted
Yes	Yes	Up to 5 years	Flotation or sale	—	—
Yes, minority	Not under normal circumstances. Nominee director only with mutual agreement	5-20 years	Redemption negotiated individually, no requirement to sell shares	18 branch offices offering wide range of advisory services	
Yes — minority	When appropriate	5-10 years	Usually by public flotation	Pro-active specialist venture capital team	£16m in 36 companies
Yes — minority (25-40%)		Equity: open. Loans: 3-6 years	Flexible in timescle and method eg, sale/ USM	Long term relationship. Seeks capital gain not running yield	£7·5m invested in 10 companies

Vehicle for capital	Backers	Capital earmarked	Type of Client or situation	Min/max funds injected	Start up capital
Innvotec Ltd Tel: (01) 245 1977	Private & institutional investors	Open	Companies capable of rapid growth. High technology development projects	£50,000+. Large amounts syndicated	Yes
INTEX Executives (UK) Limited Tel: (01) 831 6925	Private and institutional investors and trusts	Open	Industrial and commercial enterprises, especially high technology and innovation	£10,000 £1m	Yes
Lancashire & Merseyside Investment Fund Tel: Preston (0772) 264382	Public and private sector investors	£1·35m initially	Companies in Lancashire or Merseyside counties	£15,000 – £100,000	Yes
Larpent Newton & Co Ltd Tel: (01) 831 9991	Advisory work for leading UK institutions	Open	Unquoted companies requiring development capital and management buy-outs	£15,000 – £2m	Yes with experienced management
Lazard Brothers & Co Ltd Tel: (01) 588 2721	A wide range of private and institutional investors	Open	Any company with growth potential	Open	Yes
LEDU — The Small Business Agency for Northern Ireland Tel: (0232) 691031	Northern Ireland Department of Economic Development	Open	Companies employing up to 50 people in Northern Ireland	£1,500+	Loans, guarantees and grants available
Leopold Joseph & Sons Ltd Tel: (01) 588 2323	Leopold Joseph & Sons Ltd and clients	Open	Good track record, growth record, pre-tax profit over £100,00	Open	Exceptionally where previous experience and can make a sound financial contribution
London Development Capital Fund Tel: (01) 623 9333	Guinness Mahon	£6m	Companies with a track record and good management	£100,000 – £600,000	Not excluded
London Scottish Finance Corporation plc Tel: (061) 834 2861	Quoted finance company	Open	Traditional manufacturing or service companies in the north west	£25,000 – £75,000	Yes
Lorne Exploration plc Tel: Edinburgh (031) 225 9677	Private individuals	£1·5m	Venture capital for oil and gas exploration companies	£25,000 – £150,000	Yes

Rescue capital	Equity stake	Seat on board	Term of funding	Exit criteria	Special features	Portfolio
Exceptionally	Yes	In most cases	Flexible but generally 5 years	Flexible. Looking for capital growth	Active assistance to management	New fund
Yes, if viable	Usually minority only. In appropriate circumstances up to 75%	Depends upon circumstances	Equity and loan arranged according to circumstances	Not applicable	Complementary managerial and technical support and advisory services	n/a
No	Yes, 10-40%	Optional	4-8 years	Buy back options available	Equity, loan, bank guarantees or preference share packages	New fund — 2 investments
Yes	Usually	Yes	Individually tailored	Flexible	Close relationship with management. General commercial and financial advice	£12m under supervision in 20 investments
Exceptionally	Yes	As appropriate	Open	Dependent on source of funding and company	Flexible funding arrangements. Management involvement principally through Development Capital Group	75+ companies
Maintenance packages are provided	Yes	Not usually	Grants/loans/guarantees average 5 years	Repayment as required under terms and conditions of offer	Business technical, marketing and accountancy and design advice	In excess of 15,000 businesses assisted
No	Yes	Reserves the right to appoint non-executive director	Open	Listing on Stock Exchange or negotiated individually	Adaptability. Full range of financial and advisory services	Cannot be differentiated from total bank holdings
Unlikely	Always minority	Reserves the right	5-7 years	Seek realisation or marketability within fund's 10 year life	Active pursuit of deal flow through link with London local authorities	New fund
Yes	Yes — between 20% and 40%	Yes	Equity — long term. No immediate dividends required	By mutual agreement but investments expected to be long term	"Hands on" management and total management services backup	Launched 1984. 1 investment
Yes	Yes	No	Long-term	No stipulation	Oil expertise	International oil and gas companies

Vehicle for capital	Backers	Capital earmarked	Type of Client or situation	Min/max funds injected	Start up capital
Lovat Enterprise Fund Tel: (01) 621 1212	NCB Pension Funds, Legal & General, Prudential, Electra Investment Trust, Equitable Life	£7·5m	Expansion financing, mainly private companies earning £100,000+ pre-tax	£100,000 – £1m	No
Managed Technology Investors Tel: (0923) 50244	Morgan Grenfell, Prudential Assurance and PA Consulting Services	£9·1m almost all from UK institutional sources	High technology product companies, preferably established in the UK	£100,000 – £1m	Yes
Manufacturers Hanover Limited Tel: (01) 600 4585	—	Open	Development finance. Shareholder realisations including management buy-outs	£100,00 – £250,000	Will consider
Mathercourt Securities Limited Tel: (01) 831 9001	Private and institutional investors	Open	Private companies inlcuding USM, OTC and BES candidates	£25,000 – £4m syndicated as appropriate	Yes
Melville Street Investments (Edinburgh) Limited Tel: Edinburgh (031) 226 4071	Institutional investors	£18m	Profitable companies — good financial discipline — new companies — established management	£250,000 – £500,000	Yes
Meritor Investments Ltd Tel: (01) 606 2179	Midland Bank, Rolls-Royce Pension Fund	£4m	Development situations and shareholders' needs, management buy-outs	£100,00 – £250,000. May syndicate larger investments	No
Midland Bank Equity Group Tel: (01) 638 8861/ Birmingham (021) 455 8371	Midland Bank	Open	Development situations and shareholders' needs, management buy-outs	£5,000 – £2m. May syndicate larger investments	Occasionally
Montagu Investment Management Ltd Tel: (01) 626 3434	Listed investment trusts	Open	Small and medium sized companies, public or private, with growth potential	Normally £300,000 – £3m	Only occasionally
Moracrest Investments Ltd Moracrest Finance Ltd Tel: (01) 628 8409	Midland Bank, Prudential Group and British Gas Pension Fund	£15m	Development situations and shareholders' needs, management buy-outs	£200,000+. May syndicate larger investments	Occasionally

Rescue capital	Equity stake	Seat on board	Term of funding	Exit criteria	Special features	Portfolio
No	5-40%	Reserves the right to appoint non-executive director	Open	Flexible, but objective is marketability	Independent fund managed by Granville & Co. Minority equity share-holdings	12 companies – £6m
Yes	Usually substantial minority, occasionally up to 74%	Yes	Up to 1993	OTC, USM or full quote or sell back, sell out or buy out	Plays an active role in management of investee companies	£0·7m in 2 companies by end 1984
Unlikely	Yes	Yes	Open, but around 5 years preferred	Within 5 years preferred	Note — no "BES" requirement	—
Yes, where equity can replace debt	Yes, 3-40%	Normally. Often represented by experienced nominee	Tailored to suit circumstances	Flexible, but objective is marketability	Health care financing. Close working relationship with	Wide coverage; £10m funded in past three years
Yes	Minority	Retains the right to appoint a director	Long term capital	Flexible	Other merchant banking facilities available through the British Linen Bank	50 companies – £13m
No	Yes, minority	Normally	Open	Dividend flow: sale when convenient to majority shareholders	Predominantly equity investors. Loan finace as part of a package	12 companies – £3m
Takeover situations or restructuring of CTT only. Would back new management	Yes, minority	Usual in investments over £150,000	Open	Dividend flow: sale when convenient to majority share-holders	Predominantly equity investors. Loan finance as part of a package	156 companies – £47·2m (including managed funds)
No	Yes, minority	Expects the right to appoint non-executive director	Open	Basis for realisation expected 3-5 years	Flexibility	£50m unlisted US and UK
No	Yes, minority	Normally	Open	Dividend flow: sale when convenient to majority shareholders	Predominantly equity investors. Loan finance as part of a package	21 companies – £10·7m

Vehicle for capital	Backers	Capital earmarked	Type of Client or situation	Min/max funds injected	Start up capital
Rainford Venture Capital Tel: St. Helens (0744) 37227	Pilkington Bros., Prudential and others	£2·5m	Start-up or growth in North West	£50,000 – £250,000	Yes
Rothschild Ventures Limited Tel: (01) 280 5000	UK institutions	Open	Any	£100,000 upwards	Yes
Sabrelance Limited Tel: (01) 493 3599	Private and institutional investors	Open	Small and medium sized companies with OTC and USM potential	£25,000 – £500,000	Yes
Safeguard Investments Tel: (01) 283 2244	84% owned by 8 major insurance companies and pension funds	£20m	Small and medium sized UK companies	Minimum £100,000. No maximum but may syndicate over £2m	Exceptionally
Schroder Ventures Tel: (01) 382 6000	Schroder Wagg	£15m +	Venture/ development/ buy-out	£250,000 or more	Yes
Scottish Allied Investors Tel: Glasgow (041) 204 1321	James Finlay, Royal Bank Development Ltd, Stenhouse Offshore Marine	£3m	Profitable manufacturing private companies looking for expansion capital	£50,000 – £500,000	No
Scottish Development Agency Tel: Glasgow (041) 248 2700 **Small Business Division** Tel: Edinburgh (031) 343 1911	UK Government	Open	Manufacturing and service businesses operating in Scotland	Open	Yes
Scottish Offshore Investors Tel: Glasgow (041) 204 1321	James Finlay and other financial institutions	£3m	Energy related service companies with growth prospects	£50,000 – £250,000	Exceptionally
Seedcorn Capital Ltd Tel: (0272) 272250	United Kingdom Provident Institution English Association Group plc	£200,000 initially	Prototype manufacture/ research and preliminary market and small start-ups	£10,000 – £40,000 (syndication for larger sums)	Yes
Smithdown Investments Ltd Tel: (01) 408 1502 (09278) 5199	Private individuals	Open	Start-up situations and very small companies	£10,000 – £50,000	Yes

Rescue capital	Equity stake	Seat on board	Term of funding	Exit criteria	Special features	Portfolio
No	Yes	Yes	Equity plus loan if appropriate	Seeking disposal long-term loans at term	Backers provide on-going technical/managerial support	9 companies — £1·6m
Yes	Yes (always a minority)	Normally	Flexible; equity but can include preference and/or loan capital	Flexible	Constructive management support	35 companies
Yes	—	Retain the right to appoint a director	—	Flexible	Financial and advisory services provided to assist management	10 companies — £2m
Possibly	Yes — 10-40%	When appropriate	Medium to long term	Flexible	Continuing financial advice/banking finance from Close Brothers Group	Investments in 25 companies
Yes	Yes	Often	Not fixed	Sometime	Particularly interested in large management buy-outs	New fund
No	Yes, between 20-49%	Yes	Medium or long-term investment in equity or loan/equity package	Flexible — building up portfolio and not seeking to realise investment	Financial management advice and management consultancy service	6 companies — £1·3m
Exceptionally	Where appropriate	If equity taken — right to appoint non-executive director	2-20 years equity open	By agreement with other shareholders	Advisory services, ECSC low interest funds, special rates in rural areas	£33m in 791 companies
No	Yes, between 20-49%	Yes	Medium or long-term. Equity or loan/equity package	Flexible — not seeking to realise investments	Financial management advice and management consultancy service	6 companies — £2·3m
Yes	Entirely equity or equivalent	Yes	Very long term	Flexible	Will fund prototypes and provide pre-start-up funds	4 companies — £93,000
No	Normally	By agreement	Open	Open	Financial and commercial management advice etc	9 companies — £500,000

Vehicle for capital	Backers	Capital earmarked	Type of Client or situation	Min/max funds injected	Start up capital
Morris, Stewart-Brown & Co Limited *Tel:* *(01) 248 2894*	Private	Open	Small and medium size businesses, management buy-outs	Advise and syndicate for £150,000+; up to £10,000 directly	Yes
National Commercial & Glyns Limited *Tel:* *(031) 556 2555*	The Royal Bank of Scotland plc	Open	Development financing for companies with a good track record	£100,000+	No
Newmarket Company Ltd Newmarket (Venture Capital) Ltd *Tel:* *(01) 638 4551*	London listed company	Approx. $90m	Applications of new technology or innovation	Normally $200,000 – $1m, but occasionally higher	Yes, but not exclusively
Noble Grossart Investments *Tel: Edinburgh (031) 226 7011*	Noble Grossart and institutional shareholders	Unlimited	Good management in growth-"buy-out" or turnaround situations	£100,000 – £2m	Yes, if the management has good track record in previous business
Northern Investors Company *Tel: Newcastle (0623) 327068*	Industrial companies, pension funds and financial institutions	£4-6m	Companies in Northern England	£50,000 – £200,000	Yes
Oakland Management Holdings Limited *Tel: Hungerford (0488) 83555*	A leading UK institution and Business Expansion Scheme investors	£7m	Purchase of existing stakes in profitable expanding companies	£50,000 – £500,000	Yes, limited number in each portfolio
PA Developments *Tel:* *(01) 235 6060*	Two leading UK institutions	Open	Profitable private companies — capital or expansion; or purchase of existing equity	£200,000 – £1·4m	No
Pegasus Holdings Ltd *Tel:* *(01) 623 4275*	Lloyds Bank Group	Open	Proven management, pre-tax profits over £50,000 with growth potential	Minimum £100,000. No maximum, but may syndicate large investments	No
Prutec *Tel:* *(01) 828 2082*	Member of the Prudential Group	£10-15m annually	Development of high technology	Open	Yes
Pruventure *Tel:* *(01) 404 5611*	Prudential Group	Open (£15m pa)	Wide ranging approach	Typically £200,000 – £3m	Yes

Rescue capital	Equity stake	Seat on board	Term of funding	Exit criteria	Special features	Portfolio
Yes	Usually	If appropriate	Flexible to suit company	Flexible	Corporate finance and management advisory services	Commenced October 1983 — 3 companies
No	Yes — minority	Not under normal circumstances. However, the right is reserved	Up to 10 years	Flexible	Other merchant banking facilities available	26 companies — £6m
Usually for companies already invested in	Yes, but not a controlling stake	Right to appoint an independent director where appropriate	Primarily equity; no requirement for immediate income	As appropriate for long-term investor	Experience since 1972 particularly in US and UK: Worldwide contacts	US: 64 companies — $70·6m UK: 24 companies — $9·5m 4 others — $2·8m
No	Yes, usually 10-40%	Yes, with active non-executive participation	Open	Flexible	Able to contribute financial and general management skills	30 companies — £25m
Exceptionally	Minority	Reserve the right	5-7 years	Flexible	—	New fund — 1 investment to date
Yes, for growth opportunity	Yes	Yes	Flexible — up to 7 years	Flexible	Flexible investment package. Can syndicate in excess of £500,000	25 companies
No	Yes, normally 26% up to 40%	Yes	Equity preferably but will consider equity/ loan packages	Flexible — long term	Resources of PA Consulting Services	11 companies
No	Yes — usually 10-33⅓%	Reserve the right to appoint a non-executive director, but do not always exercise	Flexible	Flexible to suit company requirements	Clearing bank resources. Formulate equity/ loan packages with Lloyds branches	15 companies £5·5m
Exceptionally	Up to 40%	When appropriate	Open	To suit company and shareholders	Broad technical and financial expertise; long-term financial support	£30m plus 30 in-house development projects — £10m
Exceptionally	Always — usually in 10-30% range. Syndicate higher proportions	Usually	Open	Flexible	Prepared to take longer term view	89 companies

Vehicle for capital	Backers	Capital earmarked	Type of Client or situation	Min/max funds injected	Start up capital
Stewart Fund Managers Tel: Edinburgh (031) 226 3271	Scottish American Investment, Stewart Enterprise Investment	Open	Fast growing companies	£50,000 – £500,000	Exceptionally
The St James's Venture Capital Fund Limited Tel: (01) 493 8111	Charterhouse J. Rothschild	n/a	High technology start-up and development companies	£100,000 – £750,000	Yes
SUMIT (Sharp Unquoted Midland Investment Trust) Tel: Birmingham (021) 236 5801	Legal & General, Royal Insurance, Sun Life Assurance Society and others	£8·5m	Successful private companies and management buy-outs	£250,000 – £700,000	No
Thames Valley Ventures Limited Tel: Hungerford (0488) 83555	Oakland Management Holdings/ British Railways Pension Funds	£3m	Purchase of existing stakes in profitable expanding companies	£50,000 – £500,000	Yes, limited number in each portfolio
Thamesdale Investment Finance Co Ltd Tel: (01) 623 4097	American and European investors	Open	Small/medium sized companies. Equity and loan facilities	£25,000 upwards	Yes, in exceptional circumstances
Thomson Clive Growth Companies Fund Thomson Clive Investments Limited Tel: (01) 491 4809 (01) 409 2062	Leading UK institutions	Open	Private companies requiring capital for expansion with high quality management	Up to £300,000 (syndication for larger sums)	Exceptionally if high quality management and operations in areas of interest
Trust of Property Shares plc Tel: (01) 486 4684/ 5/6	Management support with clearing bankers	Open	Private property companies with growth potential requiring capital for expansion	£25,000 – £250,000. Syndicate for larger investments with participation	Possibly, if management of proven calibre
UKP-EA Growth Fund Ltd Tel: (01) 831 9991	United Kingdom Provident Institution and The English Association Group plc	Initially £4m	Development capital situations. Management buy-outs. Not quoted companies	£15,000 – £400,000 with access to larger sums	Only where management has successful track record in related or similar field
Venture Founders Ltd Tel: Danbury (0295) 65881	UK pension funds and insurance companies	£12m	Principally start-ups and early stage companies with growth potential	£100,000 – £600,000	Yes

Rescue capital	Equity stake	Seat on board	Term of funding	Exit criteria	Special features	Portfolio
Exceptionally	Yes, but always minority and can be part of a package	Not usually	Open	Flexible — but marketability is target	Finance packages of equity, preference and loans available	£28m in 70 investments
No	Variable (not control)	Yes	Equity or convertible debt instrument	Listing or buy-out	—	—
No	Yes, 10-35%	Yes	Open	Looking for earnings; no pressure to sell	Based in Midlands; quick decisions in principle	20 companies — £7m
Yes, for growth opportunity	Yes	Yes	Flexible up to 7 years	Flexible	Flexible investment package. Can syndicate in excess of £500,000	22 companies
Yes, if viable	Yes, 10-40%	Yes	Open	Flexible	Good overseas contacts. Facilitate export and trading situations	All activities in separate holding companies
Exceptionally	Yes, usually minority	Usually	Open	Flexible	Management support, extensive contacts particularly in US. Emphasis on technology	£20m between the two funds in UK and US
No	Yes, 10-35%	Yes	Open	Prefer dividends. Sale of equity when convenient to all shareholders	Merchant banking facilities can be introduced	Supplementary group of 6 companies
Yes	Yes, usually up to 30%. Never control	Yes	A package tailored to requirements. Loans up to 10 years	Flexible	Continuing advice and merchant banking support if required	11 companies — £2·9m
Exceptionally	Yes — prefer minority	Yes	Open	Flexible	Concentration on start-ups. Active support after investment	15 investments for two earlier funds

Vehicle for capital	Backers	Capital earmarked	Type of Client or situation	Min/max funds injected	Start up capital
S.G. Warburg & Co Ltd *Tel:* *(01) 600 4555*	A wide range of investors	Open	Any company with sufficient potential to become quoted	£100,000 – £2m generally, but no fixed maximum or minimum	Yes
Welsh Development Agency *Tel: Cardiff (0222) 32955*	UK Government	Open	Manufacturing and service industries in Wales	£2,000 – £1m	Yes
Welsh Venture Capital Fund *Tel: (0222) 32955*	Welsh Development Agency Development Capital Group and institutions	£5·6m	Companies in or coming to Wales	£50,000 – £500,000	Yes
West Midlands Enterprise Board Limited *Tel: Birmingham (021) 236 8855*	West Midlands County Council and various financial institutions	£15m	Companies employing or likely to employ 50+ in the West Midlands	£100,000 – £750,000. Syndicate larger sums	Yes
West Yorkshire Enterprise Board Ltd *Tel: Wakefield (0294) 371205*	West Yorkshire Metropolitan County Council	£5·8m	New ventures to management buy-outs	£10,000 – £500,000	Yes
E.P. Woods Investments Ltd (INCON) *Tel: (01) 242 2263*	Private and institutional investors and trusts	By arrangement with investors	Companies in industry and commerce with development and growth potential	£10,000 – £1m +	Yes

Rescue capital	Equity stake	Seat on board	Term of funding	Exit criteria	Special features	Portfolio
Yes	Yes	As appropriate	Open	To suit company and shareholders	Rapid decision making and flexible approach	35 companies, £15m invested
Only by supporting new management in takeover situation	Yes	Reserve right	5-15 years — equity open	Flexible	Range of advisory services. Outside businessmen appointed directors	250 companies — £25m
No	Always	Always	3-8 years	Public listing, or change of control	Non-financial support from Welsh Development Agency	New fund
Only if viability can be proven	Can provide a flexible package of loan/ equity capital	Take the right	Prepared to wait for a long-term capital gain	Flexible	—	—
Yes	Possibly	Possibly	Medium/ long as required	To suit client	West Yorkshire— based companies; most forms of funding available	
Yes	Yes, minority only, but flexible	Reserve right to appoint non executive director	Open	Flexible	Close and continuing relationships with management	Not stated

A Business Buyer's Checklist

Why is it for sale?

☐ Is the present owner ill?
☐ Has the business changed hands frequently?
☐ Have its profits been tumbling in recent years? Why?
☐ Is the owner selling because he wishes to retire?
☐ If so, is he the sole owner and for how long?
☐ Does retirement coincide with the expiration of the lease?
☐ Has the retiring owner's trade gradually been declining?
☐ Is his line of business intrinsically sound?
☐ Is there an expanding market for the business's product?
☐ Has the business been run with an eye to the future, rather than the past?
☐ How does the retiring owner wish to sell his business?
☐ Will payment involve the avoidance of Capital Gains Tax?
☐ Does the seller want his payments spread out over a period of time?
☐ If so, is there an arrangement for a clean transfer of control from him to you?
☐ What is the personal management 'style' of the present owner?
☐ Is the small business for sale owned by a large corporation?
☐ If so, how long have they owned it? Why did they buy it in the first place?
☐ Has the small business made a profit for its larger parent?
☐ As part of the corporation, has it continued its original business?
☐ Has the corporation sold any of the assets of the smaller business? If so, what are the reasons given?
☐ How has the corporation managed the business's employees?
☐ How have the business's accounts been handled within the corporation?
☐ Has the business been dependent upon its parent for supplies? For customers? For capital?

☐ Are you being offered a partnership in an already existing business?

☐ If so, are shares being sold? How much capital will you have to invest?

☐ Does the present owner expect you to be a 'sleeping partner' or share management with him?

☐ If you are to take an active role in the business, is there a detailed plan for the reorganisation of the management?

☐ Is the business on the market because of financial difficulties?

☐ Is it a forced sale? Is it in the hands of a receiver?

☐ Does the vendor actually own the assets you are about to buy?

☐ If the business is in receivership, will all the creditors be paid?

☐ Are any of the business's goods in the hands of third parties?

What is for sale? Who is buying it?

Sole trader

☐ If the business is owned by a sole trader, what are its assets? Which ones do you wish to buy?

☐ Is there a lease connected with the business? If so, is it assignable to a third party?

☐ Do you wish to continue trading under the business's name?

☐ What is the sole trader's reputation in the community?

☐ Does he fully own all his assets?

☐ Do you wish to retain his employees?

☐ Does the business rely on contracts which may not be transferable to third parties?

☐ Does your written agreement with the sole trader clearly identify (for tax purposes) the price of each asset you are buying?

Partnership

☐ Is the business you are contemplating buying a partnership?

☐ How many partners are there? Is one retiring?

☐ Is the sale to take place at the end of an accounting period?

☐ What will be your share of the new partnership? Will profit be shared equally?

☐ Does the new partnership agreement clearly state the amount of capital each partner is contributing?

☐ Are your new partners up to date with their tax bill?

145

☐ Does one partner have the power to negotiate for the partnership as a whole?
☐ Are you, as the purchaser, acting on behalf of a partnership? If so, will the purchase of the new business take in new partners?

Limited company
☐ Are you contemplating buying a business which is a limited company?
☐ If so, do you have a complete set of its accounts for the past few years?
☐ What is its tax position? Is it carrying any major tax liabilities?
☐ What leases or contracts has the company entered into?
☐ What are its obligations to its work force?
☐ Will a change of ownership create redundancies?
☐ What are its assets?
☐ Does it have large debtors or creditors? Are there potentially bad debts concealed in the debtors figures? Have the creditors been withheld payment in hopes of a sale?
☐ Are there potential or outstanding claims against the company for negligence or defective goods?
☐ Does it have, for tax purposes, a record of losses? If so, can they be offset against future profits?
☐ Will you be paying in cash or by issuing shares in your own larger company — or a combination of both?
☐ If you are issuing shares, will this significantly reduce your control of the company?
☐ Are you buying some, but not all, of the company for sale? If so, is it over 51 per cent?
☐ Who will be in control if you are only partially acquiring a limited company?
☐ Will you be merging the purchased business with your own company?
☐ If so, are you creating a 'group' of companies?
☐ How will the purchase of a new company affect the fortunes of your existing one?
☐ Will separate accounts be kept or will they be consolidated?
☐ Are there tax advantages to be had in keeping consolidated accounts?

Franchise

☐ Are you considering buying a franchise?

☐ If so, will you be purchasing it direct from the franchisor or from an existing franchisee? Does the franchisee have permission from the franchisor to sell the business?

☐ What is the general reputation of the franchisor's product or service? Does its level of quality meet with your approval?

☐ Have you a copy of the franchisee's latest accounts? Do they reflect a healthy and expanding business?

☐ Will the franchisor be helping you to raise capital?

☐ Do you find his management advice sound?

☐ Is the location of the franchise suitable for its product or service?

Judging the track record

☐ If the business you are thinking of buying is a sole trader or a partnership are you allowed to see the balance sheet?

☐ Does the trading account show a year-by-year increase in turnover which also allows for inflation?

☐ Is the cost of sales increasing faster than turnover?

☐ If the business is a manufacturing one, are there separate, detailed categories under cost of sales?

☐ Are wages rising faster than the value of the goods the work force produces?

☐ On what basis have the stocks been valued?

☐ What is the replacement value of the stocks?

☐ Have the stocks been over-valued?

☐ If the business is carrying heavy stocks, are they likely to become out of date or subject to changes in fashion or demand?

☐ Has the business written off the value of unsaleable goods?

☐ Has the business applied consistent criteria over the years to the valuation of its stock?

☐ What is the business's rate of stock turn? What is the average rate for the trade concerned?

☐ What is the gross profit? Is it rising or falling as a percentage of turnover?

☐ What is the net, pre-tax, profit?

☐ Are costs increasing faster than sales?

☐ Do the high administrative costs indicate a business which has become wasteful or self-indulgent?

☐ What is the relationship between costs and the sales that
result from them?

☐ Do the financial charges indicate the ratio between borrowed
money and the owner's personal financial investment in it?

☐ Is your offer of a purchase price large enough to allow the
owner to repay borrowings?

☐ What is the overall level of bad debts over a period of years?
Has the company made an allowance for bad debts in the
profit and loss accounts?

☐ What is the business's depreciation of fixed assets?

☐ Which method of depreciation − the straight line, the
reducing balance, or the revaluation − is used?

☐ Has the net profit been manipulated for tax purposes?

☐ Does it, if it is a sole trader, include the wife's earned income
allowance? If so, will you have to hire someone to replace
her?

☐ Are household expenses such as telephone and electricity
charged to the business? How do they affect the real
profitability of the business?

☐ Do travel and entertainment expenses seem unusually high?

☐ What are the fixed assets on the company's balance sheet?

☐ Has the property been revalued recently?

☐ Has depreciation enhanced past profits?

☐ What current assets appear on the balance sheet?

☐ What outstanding debts appear on the balance sheet?

☐ By dividing the debtors into the sales can you tell how long
on average it has taken the business to collect its debts? Is the
period of credit it is giving shrinking, growing or remaining
steady?

☐ What are the current liabilities of the company?

☐ What amount of credit is the business getting from its
suppliers?

☐ What is the break-up value of the business?

☐ Have you compared this year's balance sheet with those of
previous years?

☐ What is the working capital derived from deducting the
current liabilities from the current assets?

☐ What is the company's current ratio? Its liquidity ratio?

☐ How is the worth of the company divided among its owners?

☐ If the business is a partnership, what is each partner's original
investment? How much salary has each partner been
drawing?

- ☐ If the business is a limited company, what is the structure of its share capital? What classes of shares are listed in the balance sheet?
- ☐ Does a debenture appear on the balance sheet?
- ☐ Has the company's share capital been increased by a scrip issue?
- ☐ Is there a share premium account? Does the balance sheet show a capital reserve?
- ☐ If a revenue reserve is listed, what does it include?
- ☐ What is the business's rate of return on capital? Is it improving or worsening?
- ☐ How is the return on capital influenced by the 'gearing' of the business?
- ☐ If the accounts are consolidated, are you able to identify clearly each group member's contribution to profits and return on capital?
- ☐ Do the accounts include a statement showing the sources and application of funds? Have you examined the details of each? What trends emerge from a comparison of the two? Are the funds being tied up for long periods of time?
- ☐ Is there any evidence that the business is 'over-trading'?

Evaluating the assets

Property
- ☐ Is the property freehold or leasehold?
- ☐ What are its pros and cons as a home for the business you are thinking of buying? Is it the right size, conveniently laid out, located in the right place with good access to railways and roads?
- ☐ Can you get planning permission to extend the premises?
- ☐ Have you sought expert advice in estimating the current market value of the freehold property?
- ☐ If it comes to the worst and you have to sell it, will the proceeds cover your initial investment in the property?
- ☐ Is the property free of mortgages?
- ☐ Are there any restrictive covenants in the deeds?
- ☐ Does the local authority have any long-term plans for the area in which the property is situated?
- ☐ Does the present owner have planning permission to carry on his type of business?

☐ Do the buildings on the property have very specialist designs or functions? Have you had them independently surveyed?

☐ If the property is leasehold, what are the length and terms of the lease?

☐ Is the vendor, if a sole trader or a partnership, entitled to transfer the lease? Will you, in turn, as owner, be able to transfer it to a third party?

☐ What will be your liability, as a tenant, for repairs and dilapidations?

☐ Does the property's layout make it adaptable for different purposes?

☐ Will you be able to resell the lease to someone else without making a loss?

Plant and equipment

☐ Are the plant and equipment of specialised value only? Will you be able to re-sell them?

☐ Is the machinery old or obsolete? Is it about to be superseded by cheaper or improved versions?

☐ What is the machinery's current value in the second-hand market?

☐ What have the bills been for servicing or repair within the last several years?

☐ How have plant and equipment been depreciated? How much of their value remains to be written off for tax purposes?

Stock

☐ What is the current value of the stock?

☐ Are the materials overstocked, outdated, damaged or perishable?

☐ Are you buying the stock at cost or at replacement cost?

☐ How long will it take you to sell the stock?

Sales

☐ What are the past year's sales records?

☐ What are the business's debtors? When will they eventually pay up? How much is owed?

☐ What average length of credit has the vendor been extending?

☐ Is there any individual or group of customers who accounts for a disproportionate amount of the company's sales? If so, are any of them slow payers?

☐ Have you requested guarantees from the vendor against the eventuality of any debts turning bad?

Intangible assets
- ☐ Does the business contain any intangible assets — such as copyrights or patents — not included in the balance sheet?
- ☐ What is their worth if you had to put them on the market?
- ☐ Is there a 'goodwill' item in the accounts?
- ☐ Does the amount the vendor is asking for 'goodwill' balance with your assessment of the future profits of the business?

Customers and suppliers
- ☐ Who are the vendor's customers and suppliers?
- ☐ Is the business dependent upon one or two customers or suppliers? Will these remain loyal if the business is sold?
- ☐ What is the financial position of these few customers or suppliers?

The owner
- ☐ How far do the business's present reputation and success depend upon its owner?
- ☐ If the business is at all dependent upon the present owner's personality, will you be able to fill his shoes?

Staff
- ☐ Does the business for sale possess a staff?
- ☐ What is the current wage and salary bill? At what rate has it been increasing?
- ☐ What are the strengths and weaknesses of the middle management?
- ☐ Do the terms of the sale include any commitments to employees on your part?
- ☐ Do your plans for the business include any changes or cutbacks in staffing? If so, does this mean there are likely to be redundancies among the work force?
- ☐ Will you be taking over contracts of employment from the vendor?
- ☐ Are notices of redundancy and entitlement to redundancy pay the responsibility of the outgoing owner?
- ☐ Are you up to date on current employment law provisions?
- ☐ Does the vendor have service contracts with any of his employees? Will you be taking them on?
- ☐ Does the business have a private pension scheme? Is it under-funded?

What is the right price? Can you afford it?

- [ ] What are the asset values as opposed to the potential profits of the business?
- [ ] If the price demanded is based on the business's potential profits, what are the general economic climate, current rate of inflation and interest?
- [ ] What is the ratio between the amount you will have to borrow (plus interest) and the purchase price?
- [ ] How will high inflation affect the future profits of the business?
- [ ] Is the vendor over-valuing both his assets and future profits?
- [ ] Is there a gap between the asset value of the business and its profitability value?
- [ ] Have you prepared a cash flow forecast for the next year which establishes the peak requirement for cash?
- [ ] Does this forecast include new stock, supplies, salaries, corporation tax, overhead, rates or rent?
- [ ] How much working capital will you need?
- [ ] What hidden costs are involved in actually making the purchase?
- [ ] What will your accountants and solicitors charge?
- [ ] If you are buying shares in a limited company, what stamp duty will be payable?
- [ ] How much money of your own can you invest in the business? How much will you have to borrow? What is the ratio between the two?
- [ ] What is the return on investment?
- [ ] What interest are you likely to be paying?
- [ ] Is the gearing high or low? If high, what is the risk?
- [ ] How much is future inflation likely to eat into your profits?
- [ ] Will the value of your assets keep pace with inflation?
- [ ] What proportion of your profits will have to go back into the business in order to keep up with inflation?
- [ ] Have the present owners taken such a consideration into account in past years?
- [ ] What wage will you yourself be drawing from your new business?
- [ ] If you are buying a company, what was the previous owner drawing by way of salary and dividends?
- [ ] If you are buying a sole trader or partnership, have you considered that you will be taxed on the business's profits — not on the cash you actually receive?

☐ Have you included the cost of National Insurance stamps in your calculations?

☐ Will you be investing in a private pension scheme?

☐ Have you allowed for the incidental expenses that can arise if you are moving out of employment to self-employment?

☐ Are you entering final negotiations for the sale of the business with a firm view about its value to you?

☐ Do you have an upper limit in mind? Is it your starting point? Is your first offer so low as to be derisory?

☐ What do you conclude about the vendor's like/dislike of haggling over small details?

☐ What is the vendor's attitude to negotiating?

☐ Do you have competitors in the negotiations for the sale of the business?

☐ Will you be able to set the agenda for the negotiations?

☐ Will your lawyers and/or accountants be present?

Paying for it

☐ Will you be asking your bank for an overdraft to cover the purchase of the business?

☐ If so, what is your bank's current base rate of interest? How much more than base rate will they charge you?

☐ What is your forecast of future interest rates? If they increase, how will this affect your cash flow?

☐ Can your business be expected to generate sufficient profits to pay the interest charges and reduce the borrowing steadily in the short- to medium-term future?

☐ What is the ratio between your funds invested and the bank overdraft?

☐ What form of security will you be offering the bank in exchange for overdraft facilities?

☐ Will your bank give you a loan? If so, will the business be able to make repayments according to the schedule?

☐ Have you asked your bank manager for advice concerning other sources of venture capital his institution might offer?

☐ Will you be mortgaging your house or other private property to raise capital?

☐ If you have found a partner to invest in the business, is the arrangement in writing?

☐ If you are borrowing privately from a friend or relation, does your written agreement deal with the eventuality of his or her death?

☐ If the business you want to buy is a limited company, have you considered selling some shares to raise capital?

☐ Are you seeking long-term loan capital in the form of a debenture?

☐ What share of the company's equity will you own? Is it at least 51 per cent? 76 per cent?

☐ Have you drawn up a proposal to circulate to institutions which provide long-term investment capital? How many such institutions will you contact?

☐ Have you hired an accountant or stockbroker to approach the institutions for you? If so, are the terms of their fees clear?

☐ Have you investigated sources of funding from central and local government?

☐ Can you raise capital by selling off any of the assets without reducing the business's value?

Appendix

Useful addresses

Advisory, Conciliation and Arbitration Service (ACAS), Head Office, 11-12 St James's Square, London SW1Y 4LA

Agricultural Mortgage Corporation Ltd, Bucklersbury House, 3 Queen Victoria Street, London EC4N 8DU

Alliance of Small Firms and Self Employed People, 42 Vine Road, East Molesey, Surrey KT8 9LF

Association of British Chambers of Commerce, Sovereign House, 212a Shaftesbury Avenue, London WC2H 8EW

Association of Independent Businesses, Europe House, World Trade Centre, London E1 9AA

Association of Invoice Factors, 109-13 Royal Avenue, Belfast BT1 1FF

British Franchise Association, Franchise Chambers, 75a Bell Street, Henley-on-Thames, Oxon RG9 2BD

British Institute of Management, Small Firms Information Service, Management House, Cottingham Road, Corby, Northamptonshire NN17 1TT

British Insurance Association, Aldermary House, Queen Street, London EC4 4JD

British Overseas Trade Board (BOTB), 1 Victoria Street, London SW1H 0ET

Companies Registration Office, Companies House, 55 City Road, London EC1Y 1BB

Confederation of British Industry (CBI), Smaller Firms Council, Centre Point, New Oxford Street, London WC1A 1DD

Department of Commerce, Chichester House, 43-7 Chichester Court, Belfast BT1 4PJ

Department of Trade and Industry, Ashdown House, 1 Victoria Street, London SW1H 0ET

Equipment Leasing Association, 18 Upper Grosvenor Street, London W1X 9PB

Export Credits Guarantee Department, Information Section, Aldermanbury House, London EC2 2EL

Finance Houses Association, 18 Upper Grosvenor Street, London W1X 9PB

Investors in Industry, 91 Waterloo Road, London SE1 8XP

London Chamber of Commerce, 69 Cannon Street, London EC4 5AB. Business Registry offers advice, certificate of registration, and search facilities.

Office of Fair Trading, Field House, Breams Buildings, London EC4A 1PR

Registrar of Companies, Companies House, Crown Way, Maindy, Cardiff CF4 3UZ

Registrar of Companies for Scotland, 102 George Street, Edinburgh EH2 3DJ

Further reading

An A-Z of Employment and Safety Law, Peter Chandler (Kogan Page)

Buying a Shop, A St J Price (Kogan Page)

Croner's Reference Book for the Self-employed and Smaller Business (Croner Publications)

Guardian Guide to Running a Small Business, The, 4th edn, ed Clive Woodcock (Kogan Page)

Law and Practice of Franchising, The, Martin Mendelsohn and Arthur Nicholson (Franchise Publications)

Law for the Small Business, 4th edn, Patricia Clayton (Kogan Page)

Management Buy Outs, special report no. 115 (The Economist)

Money for Business and *Money for Export* (Bank of England: Bulletin Group, Economic Intelligence Unit)

Pensions for the Self-employed, Mark Daniel (The Sunday Telegraph)

Raising Finance: the Guardian Guide for the Small Business, 2nd edn, Clive Woodcock (Kogan Page)

Small Business Guide, The, Colin Barrow (BBC Publications)

Taking up a Franchise, 3rd edn, Godfrey Golzen and Colin Barrow (Kogan Page)

Understand Your Accounts, 2nd edn, A St J Price (Kogan Page)

VAT Made Easy, A St J Price (Kogan Page)

Working for Yourself: the Daily Telegraph Guide to Self-employment, 8th edn, Godfrey Golzen (Kogan Page)

Index

Index of Advertisers